Graham Handley MA PHD

Brodie's Notes on William Golding's

Lord of the Flies

Pan Educational London and Sydney

First published by James Brodie Ltd
This edition published 1976 by Pan Books Ltd,
Cavaye Place, London SW10 9PG

18   19   20

© Graham Handley 1965
ISBN 0 330 50017 1
Printed and bound in Great Britain by
Richard Clay Ltd, Bungay, Suffolk

Contents

To the student

Lord of the Flies was first published in 1954, and since then has gone into many editions, both in this country and in America. It is a book used widely in schools, and has been and is still set by examining boards in this country. It would almost certainly be true to say that it is the most discussed novel of the past ten years; it has been filmed, programmes on radio and television have been devoted to it, while Christians and humanists have acclaimed it, and other Christians and humanists have condemned it, its theme and (supposed) conclusions, at least.

Why has *Lord of the Flies* made such a stir? The answer is, in part, owing to the nature of the society in which we live. William Golding has placed a group of small boys, aged between five or six and twelve, on an island, and has demonstrated how he thinks they would behave. He has defined his conception in this way:

> I see, or I bring myself to see, a certain set of circumstances in a particular way. If it is the way everybody else sees them, there is no point in writing a book.

Our society would not like to think of its children in the way that Mr Golding sees them. Yet he sees them for what they are, he sees quite clearly how thin is the veneer on many of them – and us – and perhaps he looks back to the times he lived and fought through in the Second World War – the times of racial persecution and atrocities, massive and uncompromising instances of man's inhumanity to man which still fester in the 'peaceful' world of today. *Lord of the Flies* is an exposition and an exposure of human nature. It is truthful and it is compassionate; it is uncompromising and it is human. Those boys who follow Jack are naked except for the paint of their new existence; Ralph, Piggy and Simon are clothed in the memory of civilised behaviour, and they do not shed their clothes, despite the temptations. It is possible, therefore, to regard the novel as pessimistic or optimistic, either as a tribute to mankind's clinging to civilized codes (as in Ralph, Piggy, Simon) or an indictment of mankind's facile return to savagery. In an age of materialism which displays little concern for a serious way of life, where an acquisitive society values goods above morality, and where the superficial has already replaced the reality of living, *Lord of the Flies* might be expected to shock. That it has done so is a tribute to the power of the author's writing, and to his comprehensive and intuitive understanding of children – 'intuitive' because the description of how the boys behave requires a forecasting imagination. Yet no one who has read the book can doubt the authenticity of their reactions and experiences, or that the truism 'the child is father of the man' is valid for all time.

The aim of this book of notes is to send you, the reader, to the text of *Lord of the Flies*, and it is in no sense a substitute for that text. If you are reading the novel in school, either as a class reader or for an examination, do not forget that it is your response and your conclusions, based on intelligent reading, which are important. You may see in it some clue to the behaviour of a minority of today's 'teenagers', you may find in it some valid pronouncements on the kind of world or society in which we live, you may consider its moral or spiritual overtones, or you may read it for what it undeniably is – a good story superbly told, full of tension, excitement and fear. Above all, treat the book as all books should be treated by their readers, namely, as an experience. Read with an awareness of the power of words to create this imaginative experience for you, for a book like *Lord of the Flies*, which is both profound and vital, can only deepen and enrich the lives of its readers.

There is much critical material on *Lord of the Flies*, amongst which the following have been found particularly stimulating: Peter Green's *The World of William Golding* (*A Review of English Literature*, April 1960) and C. B. Cox's *The Lord of the Flies* (*Critical Quarterly*, Vol. II, No. 2, Summer 1960). In addition there are readable chapters on William Golding in F. R. Karl's *A Reader's Guide to the Contemporary English Novel* (Thames and Hudson) and J. J. Gindin's *Postwar British Fiction* (Cambridge University Press).

For this short study the text of the Penguin Modern Classics edition of *Lord of the Flies* has been used, and all page references in the Notes are to that edition. Chapter references are given as well, however, so that the Notes may be used with any edition of the text.

The film

Students can be strongly recommended to see Peter Brook's film of *Lord of the Flies*. This sticks closely to the book, at least as far as the dialogue is concerned, and it serves to underline Golding's fine sense of the conversational exchanges between boys. The production makes no concessions to the squeamish, and the only major omission is Simon's mystical experience with the lord of the flies, the pig's head on a stick. Ralph, Piggy and Jack are superbly portrayed, and at times the performances of the actors capture the terrible atmosphere which runs through the novel. Simon is photogenically excellent, but there is perhaps a general failure to convey the quality of his sainthood. There are one or two effective departures from the book, perhaps the most notable being at the end, where no dialogue is spoken between Ralph and the naval officer; instead the camera focuses expressively on the moving silence of Percival. The photography throughout is excellent, and the heat, the fear, the terrifying changes with their tragic results, are powerfully conveyed. There is no attempt at sensationalism or distortion, and the overall effect is that of a sensitive, thoroughly sympathetic rendering of the novel.

The author

William Golding was born in 1911 in a small Cornish village, and his early childhood thus coincided with the First World War. He was educated at Marlborough Grammar School, going on from there to Brasenose College, Oxford, where he read English. He graduated in 1933, afterwards becoming a teacher. He was married in 1939. In 1940 he joined the navy, and during the next five years he saw much action at sea, witnessing the sinking of the *Bismarck* and taking part in the D-Day landings on the French coast. He left the navy in 1945, and resumed teaching at Bishop Wordsworth's School, Salisbury, where he remained until 1962. He enjoys sailing, and as a recreation taught himself classical Greek. He visits Greece whenever it is possible, and has lectured in the United States. A widely-known author, who has travelled much, he yet shuns the public gaze and tries to avoid publicity. He believes that 'The book's the thing, independent of the author'.

Since the publication of *Lord of the Flies*, William Golding has written four other novels and a play, *The Brass Butterfly* (1958). The novels are: *The Inheritors* (1955), *Pincher Martin* (1956), *Free Fall* (1959), *The Spire* (1964). No examination of the themes or brief indications of the techniques Golding employs in these works can do justice to his achievement. He is concerned with innocence, with evil, with retribution; with the state of man, with the mind of man. He has said himself that he has turned his back on the contemporary literary scene, and certainly his novels are like no others being written at the present time. Each one is original, vivid and compelling, and although they are linked by the exploration of themes which have much in common, they are in no sense a re-working. There is no overlapping; there is only expansion.

The book

Source

R. M. Ballantyne's nineteenth-century boys' adventure story – a classic of its kind – can truly be called the starting point of *Lord of the Flies*. Instead of delving into the parallels in detail (although some are mentioned in passing) it has been thought best to summarize the main outlines of Ballantyne's story, so that students of *Lord of the Flies* can draw their own conclusions as to how Golding is using the material of the original. Perhaps the highest tribute one can pay Golding, however, is to say that a reader unfamiliar with *The Coral Island* will not be inhibited in any sense from a full appreciation of the power of *Lord of the Flies*. The latter is human, literary and artistic; *The Coral Island* is escapist entertainment, undistinguished in style or content, though interesting both for its moral tone and for a certain naïveté.

The story of *The Coral Island* is told in the first person by the hero Ralph (equivalent to the Ralph of *Lord of the Flies*, whose surname is never given), a boy of fifteen who has always had a passion to go to sea. His two companions on a voyage to the South Seas are Jack Martin, 'a tall, strapping, broad-shouldered youth of eighteen' and Peterkin Gay, a boy of fourteen who is 'little, quick, funny, decidedly mischievous'. These two approximate in the loosest way to Jack and Simon in *Lord of the Flies*. The boys are shipwrecked on a coral island, and immediately start to fend for themselves. They have many adventures, and live for a time on the tropical fruit and vegetables available, as well as fish and oysters. They soon discover traces of man and of animals, but their first major encounter is with a shark. After this, Jack persuades the others to explore the whole island, one of his reasons being that their need is to find some animal food.

They make bows and arrows and clubs, spears and slings. They find some pigs, but these get away, though Peterkin, who has gone off on his own, has succeeded in spearing a piglet.

They have their first real feast on this, a vegetable called the taro-root, and a wood pigeon. Next they encounter what appears to be a wild-cat, though in fact it is a practically starving domestic one; shortly after this they discover a dilapidated hut, in which they find the skeleton of a man and a dog. There is an old pistol which they remove for their own use. After an exploration of a place called Diamond Cave, they kill a large sow and transfix the animal on a stick, lugging it back to their bower for a feast. Later the boys make a small boat and explore some of the minute adjacent islands.

Their next adventure is with two parties of raiding natives, one being pursued on to the island by the other. Thanks to the heroism of Jack, the boys rescue an important chief, Tararo, and a beautiful girl, Avatea. The natives depart happily, and shortly after this the boys see the sail of a schooner coming towards the island. On closer inspection this proves to be a pirate ship, and the boys take to the underwater cavern and hide. Ralph emerges, thinking the pirates have gone, and is immediately seized, brutally bound, and flung on board the pirates' boat.

The Captain, however, pretends that he is not a pirate but a sandal-wood trader; he is gradually impressed by Ralph's forthrightness and courage, and the boy becomes an active member of the crew, making friends with one of the better type of cut-throats, whose nickname is Bloody Bill. Ralph discovers how the Captain treats the natives, whether they have been converted to Christianity or not. He is a ruthless profiteer.

Eventually they come to an island, where the Captain negotiates with the chief, Romata, for wood-cutting rights, and here Ralph meets his old friend Tararo. He learns from him that Avatea, the Samoan girl the boys had earlier saved, has upset Tararo by falling in love with a native chief (later, we learn, converted to Christianity) whom Tararo hates. Shortly afterwards Ralph overhears a conversation between the Captain and the mate in which it is apparent that the Captain intends to raid and betray the natives, sailing the schooner close to the shore and bringing his heavy gun to bear on them. Ralph tells Bill of the plan, and they arrange to thwart it.

They succeed. The Captain and many of the crew are captured and killed, and in the fight Bill is wounded. He and Ralph alone get back to the schooner, and Bill later dies of his wounds. Ralph, managing the schooner himself, gets back to the coral island and is reunited with Jack and Peterkin. Jack chivalrously wishes to find Avatea and see to it that she is made happy by marrying the man she loves. They make for the island, reach it, treat with the natives on behalf of Avatea with the help of a missionary, and are eventually taken by the natives and imprisoned. They wait for death but, to their surprise, are released by the tribe, who have just been converted to Christianity. All ends happily, and Avatea marries her young Christian chief.

The interested student may wish to follow the path taken by some literary critics, and explore *The Coral Island* itself. Much time could be spent seeking out contrasts and parallels – like the killing of a pig, or the practical aptitude of each set of boys (perhaps hardly valid, in view of the difference in age between each group) – but one thing must be kept in mind. Although *Lord of the Flies* has been called a fable, the reactions of the boys are a study in realism, imaginative realism perhaps, which is profoundly pessimistic in its implications. There is no realism in *The Coral Island*, but the unreality of boys, natives and pirates all reflect the passive optimism of the author.

Title
The Lord of the Flies. Beelzebub. (From the Arabic 'Baal-Zebub', the fly-lord). The Geneva Bible of 1560, followed by the Authorized of 1611, represents the Old Testament word exactly as 'Baal-zebub'. From the New Testament designation of Beelzebub as 'prince of demons', the word becomes at an early period one of the popular names of the Devil. Milton used it as the name of one of the fallen angels. The pig's head holds dominion over all the subject flies, just as the beast or evil within the boys holds dominion over their actions.

Plot

The plot is straightforward and the details are given in the summaries for each chapter. The boys, plane-wrecked on an island, elect a chief, and at first live amicably. But soon differences arise among them as to the priorities, they have nightmares and fears, and eventually the society splits into two sections – those who hunt and who become savages and kill, those, eventually only Ralph, who believe in rational conduct and the codes of civilization.

Just as Ralph is about to be killed by the savages, a naval officer arrives with a rescue party.

Chapter headings

These are for the most part self-explanatory. Chapter One is called *The Sound of the Shell*, a direct reference to the conch which is used to call the assemblies, and is therefore the symbol of law and order. *Fire on the Mountain*, Chapter Two, ends with the fire that the boys have lit getting out of hand. Chapter Three, *Huts on the Beach*, carries a certain irony, for the huts are constructed only by a few, and one hut, at least, collapses. Chapter Four, *Painted Faces and Long Hair*, indicates the first manifestation of savagery, and Chapter Five, *Beast from Water*, the superstitions which lead to the inward fears which spark off savagery. Chapter Six is called *Beast from Air*, the irony being that the sign for which Ralph asked from the world of grown-ups is the dead parachutist who testifies that civilization is in ruins, just as the boys' society is in ruins. Chapter Seven, *Shadows and Tall Trees*, refers to the search for the beast through the forest, and Chapter Eight, *Gift for the Darkness*, is the pig's head offered to the beast (with an ironic look forward to the 'darkness of man's heart' which Ralph weeps for at the end). Chapter Nine is *A View to a Death*, the view of the Lord of the Flies and the dead parachutist, and the death of Simon. Chapter Ten, *The Shell and the Glasses*, is overlaid with irony. Jack does not come to steal the shell but Piggy's glasses, which will make fire; Piggy loses his glasses (and therefore his sight), but the conch remains, the symbol of rational sight. Chapter

Eleven, *Castle Rock*, is ironic in that the Chief has turned a natural bastion into a fort for his savages and Chapter Twelve, *Cry of the Hunters*, is the ululation which the savages hope will lead them to Ralph, their most important kill.

Background

Strictly speaking, this section, brief though it is, should be called *foreground* and *background*. The foreground is the island, described paradisaically and realistically by Golding, against which is enacted the tragedy of little boys becoming little savages, while the background is the civilization they have rejected and forgotten in their lust for blood. The theme of the book is that human beings are removed from savagery only by the restraints of civilization, applied in the first place by grown-ups in authority over children.

Characters

The characters in *Lord of the Flies* are a group of English schoolboys using the slang and jargon common to their time (i.e. at some period in the nineteen-fifties), and possessing recognizable traits which make them individuals. Since William Golding is describing a community of children with adult readers in mind, the credibility of the characters is a prerequisite; but, in addition, they have to be made convincing in an *imaginary* situation, and this is Golding's particular achievement. Although many of the characters exhibit adult traits, we are never allowed to forget that they are schoolboys who have, with the exception of Ralph, Piggy and Simon, gone wild. It is very tempting to attach a label to each of the characters and to measure him by a moral yardstick, or even to stress the salient characteristic in each – martyrdom in Simon, dictatorship in Jack, democracy in Ralph. But the success of characterization in literature usually depends on development, and *Lord of the Flies* is no exception. At the beginning of our acquaintance with each of the characters we are given certain hints about them – Ralph's capacity for dreaming, Piggy's need to be accepted, Jack's domineering desire to assert himself,

Simon's withdrawn and timid nature. But by the end of the novel the potential of each on their complexity as well as their simplicity. It has been said that it is possible to read *Lord of the Flies* on certain levels – as a myth or fable, as a finely written story, as an allegory of our times, or as a study of human nature. The editor believes that it is a comprehensive investigation of children's minds and their outward reactions, a searching evaluation of human conduct. In an interview, Golding once said, 'I think it is, in fact, a realistic view of the Ballantyne situation'. Nowhere is his realism more apparent than in his delineation of character.

Ralph

'Which is better, law and rescue, or hunting and breaking things up?'

In a purely conventional novel Ralph would be called the hero. In a book which contains Simon, who sacrifices himself for others, and Piggy, who is unquestionably Ralph's intellectual peer, it is difficult to 'place' Ralph according to accepted terminology. He is the central character, however, and many of the events, reactions and descriptions are seen through his eyes or set down as if they are from his consciousness. He is twelve years old and impressive physically, but when we first meet him we are told that 'there was a mildness about his mouth and eyes that proclaimed no devil', and this is to be demonstrated as the story progresses. His early reactions are those of a boy determined to make the most of this unexpected freedom from adult supervision. He does not see people so much as things, and his first reception of Piggy is one of ridicule; though this is not unkindly meant, it takes many experiences and conversations to make Ralph see Piggy as a person. When he is particularly elated in their early days on the island, Ralph stands on his head, turns cartwheels, or indulges in mock fights; yet he is the natural chief, owing to his stillness, his size and, of course, the possession of the conch. He owes much to Piggy (including the conch), but for the most part he reasons clearly, needing to be alone to think things out. He tells Piggy that his father is a commander in the navy, and he seems to have inherited a sense of authority. He realizes that as chief he is going to be resented by Jack, and is prepared to appease the latter by giving him his hunters, though he has no conception (until he throws a spear at a boar when they are searching for the beast) of the extent of Jack's mania. His own sense of priorities shows how fitted he is to be a leader; rescue (despite the delight of freedom) and shelter are his main concern. He is responsible and can organize, and he establishes rules for assemblies which ensure that anyone who wishes to speak will be given the opportunity. Above all, he is balanced; he does not believe in ghosts or beasts, and he does not allow himself to be distracted into playing games when there is business to be attended to. He has what the author defines as 'the directness of genuine leadership'.

Ralph's tolerance and open-mindedness is in a sense his undoing. He does not understand Simon, but he appreciates his capacity for trying to help with the shelters; he does not readily appreciate Piggy, but he acknowledges Piggy's common sense and, later, his wisdom. His 'lack of devil' means that he will not resort to violence when most of the other boys have done so; his passionate sense of responsibility alienates those who live for the moment. When Ralph becomes chief he realizes at once the need for adult behaviour and this, thrust upon him, means that he can never view things as some of the others do. His first real crisis is when he discovers that Jack and his hunters have let out the fire, although earlier he has been incensed by Jack's inability to put the building of shelters before the hunting of pigs with wooden spears. Ralph's sense of loss when the ship recedes in the distance is acute:

Ralph ran stumbling along the rocks, saved himself on the edge of the pink cliff, and screamed at the ship. 'Come back! Come back!'

He ran backwards and forwards along the cliff, his face always to the sea, and his voice rose insanely. 'Come back! Come back!' (Chapter IV, p.65).

In a moment of weakness he grins when Jack imitates Piggy, but he is uncompromising in refusing to accept an 'English' apology for Jack's irresponsibility; yet Ralph was not born for self-denial, and he accepts the meat which Jack has brought them.

His summoning of an assembly after the feast is characteristic, for Ralph possesses moral courage and although he makes himself unpopular with some of the boys, he does not hesitate to assert what is right and what they should do. When he has heard Jack call the littluns cowards for their fear, when he has seen that the majority of the boys believe in ghosts, an awareness of their state comes to him:

The world, that understandable and lawful world, was slipping away. Once there was this and that; and now – and the ship had gone (V. 87).

When Jack asserts the power of the hunters and leads the majority off for the first time, Ralph is cautious, and the little boy in him wishes for a 'sign or something' from the world of grown-ups. When that sign appears to be a beast, Ralph agrees to go on the hunt, but with typical concern for others, thinks of the littluns and the need to protect them. His single-mindedness is admirable:

'Hasn't anyone got any sense? We've got to re-light that fire. You never thought of that, Jack, did you? Or don't any of you want to be rescued?' (VI. 98).

In fact so determined is Ralph on being rescued, that his ideas refuse to come clearly or logically, as the strain grows more intense, and as the boys become more savage and less amenable to rational suggestion. The need to think for others taxes his concentration:

A strange thing happened in his head. Something flittered there in front of this mind like a bat's wing, obscuring his idea (VI. 103).

This is to recur many times before they are rescued.

Although he admits to fear, Ralph is not lacking in courage. He climbs the mountain and sees what he thinks is the beast. But Jack is now determined to oust Ralph or go off on his own, and Ralph has soon to face the fact that nearly all the biguns have deserted him. Pathetically he discusses the situation with Piggy – 'What makes things break up like they do?' – a boyish acknowledgment of what he feels is his own inadequacy. He witnesses the murders of Piggy and Simon, but clings to sanity and the codes of civilization to the end. As the savagery builds up, so Ralph dreams more of home, though home in sleep can have nightmarish associations. When the small group go to Castle Rock, he feels the need to assert his chieftainship over them, and almost quarrels with Piggy in so doing. After Jack's triumph he is hunted like a pig; his anguish is made immediate to us by Golding, for frequently the reactions and promptings are from his inner voice;

> Break the line.
> A tree.
> Hide, and let them pass (XII. 187).

But Ralph *is* a natural leader, and when the naval officer arrives he states his leadership and does what talking there is to do. He has seen his ideals crushed and evil triumph, and in his suffering he breaks down and cries.

Ralph represents the boy of character and sensitivity (this latter quality develops as he comes to know his companions better) who tries to face in an adult way a situation which, because of the 'darkness of man's heart', is beyond him. He has integrity, compassion, courage and authority, and a strong awareness of the values of the civilization the boys have left. He battles for what is good and right against what is wrong and evil. He fails, and although that failure is circumstantial rather than absolute, so uncompromising and human have his moral assertions been, that we feel in his failure the failure of mankind to deal with the forces of evil.

Jack
He tried to convey the compulsion to track down and kill that was swallowing him up.

Jack is the natural antithesis to Ralph yet, were it not for

Piggy and Simon, one feels that he and Ralph would be capable of compromizing. Jack makes it clear that he has no time or sympathy for Simon, and he has a personal antipathy to Piggy. Jack is used to power, and exerts a prefect-cum-regimental authority over the choir. He has the senior boy and adult preference for the use of surnames as against Christian names; in fact it is one of the marks of his superficial maturity, like his easy use of slang and his daring use of swear words. His salient characteristic is aggression, and he has an overmastering urge to lead; later this urge is wedded to a need to kill, and thus assert his chieftainship through his superior hunting prowess.

Jack has a claim – which he is not slow to state – to be chief. Since one of his later gibes at Ralph is that he is not a prefect, we imagine that Jack is. He is self-confident and fluent, arrogant and inconsiderate of others. Simon's faints do not move him, he has no concern for the littluns, and at one point says, albeit jokingly, that if there were a shortage of pigs they would have to kill a littlun. He is irresponsible in the extreme, letting the fire go out while he indulges his obsession for pig-hunting, wantonly breaking up serious discussion by making funny remarks. Despite his appearance and age, he is a little boy in the sense that he has to play games and is incapable of rational thought, at least sustained rational thought. He asserts the superiority of the British, and he is an example of the type of very limited Englishman, the type who does not wish to think, and whose standards have been fashioned for him by the limited society in which he lives. In a way he is like the naval officer who leads the rescue (not that the naval officer is evil in any sense) in so far as his horizons are limited, his responses conditioned.

When Simon faints, we are told that 'Merridew, his eyes staring, made the best of a bad job'. There is a constant reference throughout the book to Jack's eyes, regularly described as 'mad', 'bolting', 'opaque', and this cannot fail to produce in the reader a feeling of revulsion, a feeling that Jack is not normal. Frequently we find him on the edge of hysteria:

He spun on his heel, centre of a bewildered circle of boys. 'I got you meat!'

Numberless and inexpressible frustrations combined to make his rage elemental and awe-inspiring. 'I painted my face – I stole up. Now you eat – all of you – and I – ' (IV. 71).

Jack is not at this point chief – moreover, he has just been reprimanded by Ralph for neglecting the fire – and this is the kind of violent reaction which is going to lead to even more action later. Jack is a bully, and this is shown by his treatment of Piggy. He uses Piggy's glasses to light the fire, taking them by force, and when he is particularly incensed he smacks Piggy's head. He is always ridiculing him and raising cheap laughs at his expense. The potential killer and dictator is early revealed. At first we feel that it may be merely bravado:

He snatched his knife out of the sheath and slammed it into a tree trunk . . . He looked round fiercely, daring them to contradict (1.31).

In fact he becomes skilled at his trade, a little boy practised beyond his years in the processes of slaughter:

Jack began to clean his bloody hands on the rock. Then he started work on the sow and paunched her, lugging out the hot bags of coloured guts, pushing them into a pile on the rock while the others watched him (VIII. 130).

But this is mechanical compared with the tortures he allows Roger to perform on the twins, or his arbitrary beating of Wilfred. We see in Jack the abuse of power, and this is linked to the little boy's fear of the unknown. He has to make a sacrifice to the beast, for his superstition is much more powerful than his reason, and his superstition prepares the way for his observance of ritual. Seen from one angle Jack is ludicrous:

Jack was waiting for something. He whispered urgently to the others.

'Go on – now!'

The two savages murmured. Jack spoke sharply.

'Go on!'

The two savages looked at each other, raised their spears together and spoke in time.

'The Chief has spoken.'

Then the three of them turned and trotted away (VIII. 134).

If the results were not so terrible this would be funny. But having assumed the mask and the paint – having covered himself thus, as Golding says, freeing himself from shame and self-consciousness – Jack is at liberty to indulge those tendencies which have been latent in him, or which have in the past been subject to the rules of society and consequently kept within bounds. The little boy in him runs away crying with humiliation when, following an emotional appeal to the assembly after the hunting of the beast, he is apparently rejected by the boys. Most of the latter join him, however, for his philosophy of life can be summed up in his own words, 'Who'll join my tribe and have fun?' (IX. 143).

This is his sincere assessment of what he stands for, but by a terrible irony, a tragic flaw in his character makes him stand for ritualistic murder. Jack begins by killing to justify himself to Ralph and the other boys, but he ends by turning to ritual and murder whenever he wishes or whenever anything occurs which requires thought, or balance, or return to the standards of civilization. Thus, when Ralph points out to him that, clever though the hunters are, they have made no shelters and a thunderstorm is beginning, he appeals, facilely, to the primitive instincts he himself has stirred up in the boys, 'Do our dance! Come on! Dance!' (IX. 144).

This is the demented urging of the demagogue, and what he starts ends in the murder of Simon. Always given to cunning, he now becomes hypocritical, denying that the beast has been killed, and saying that it came disguised, warning his tribesmen that it may appear again. Jack does not display guilt, and the next killing, though engineered by Roger, drives him to an insane assertion and threat:

'See? See? That's what you'll get! I meant that! There isn't a tribe for you any more! The conch is gone . . .' Viciously, with full intention, he hurled his spear at Ralph (XI. 172).

He is now a primitive chief, imitating everything that he considers such a chief would do. Thus, in the final onslaught on Ralph on the beach, when the naval officer finds them, he is wearing one of his trophies, Piggy's glasses, at his waist.

The character of Jack shows how, given certain tendencies in a new set of conditions, where there are no restrictions from adults, the primitive desires and actions are released, and there is consequently a reversion to a primitive type. Apart from his black cap, Jack loses everything he had in civilization; he replaces his leadership of the choir, based on seniority and the exercise of arbitrary power, by the chieftainship of a tribe, based on arbitrary power (including torture and murder) and a lust for blood which is to be satisfied by hunting. No moral standards interfere to slow his movement towards complete depravity.

Piggy
'What are we? Humans? Or animals? Or savages? What's grown ups going to think?'

There is a suspicion at first that Piggy is a caricature, a kind of Billy Bunter cast up on the shore for everyone to laugh at. Piggy does provide amusement for the boys – he is easy to ridicule, constantly refers to his 'ass-mar' and his auntie, is fat and apprehensive of anything involving physical activity, and he talks too much. We are told that the boys regard him as an outsider, not because of his different accent or his asthma, but because of his disinclination for manual work. In the first instance Piggy is pathetic, and his meeting with Ralph sufficiently underlines his own realization that he is an outsider, one who finds it difficult to be accepted by other boys. This pathos is further stressed by his tendency to see what he wishes to see – that is, when Ralph smiles at him on one occasion he misinterprets it as friendliness. Ralph is really smiling with delight at the contemplation of the island as a place on which to play and have fun until they are rescued. But Piggy is the kind of out-sider who has acquired valuable knowledge, doubtless because he has been thrown on his own resources so much. He provides Ralph with information about the conch, and is thus indirectly responsible for the summoning of the first assembly. And here he makes himself at once useful, for he goes around collecting the names of the children – though he never gets a complete list. He is let down, in his own estimation, by Ralph, who tells the others that his name is Piggy, though Ralph would not have known this unless Piggy himself had told him. Thus Piggy helps his torturers.

Piggy clings passionately to Ralph ('I was with him when he found the conch'), not only because Ralph accepts him more than the others do, but because he recognizes the quality of Ralph's leadership, and unobtrusively fills the gaps in Ralph's reasoning when he can. Any pressure of emotional feeling, however, brings on an asthmatic attack; and we notice too, how dependent Piggy is on his glasses, for without them he can only see a 'luminous wall'. Hence his terror when Jack snatches them from him to light a fire. But his inward sight, so to speak, is more than compensation, for with it he sees the situation of himself and his companions much more clearly than they do. Unfortunately, his physical disadvantages make him fearful of assault, and Jack is quick to discover this. Yet, although fearful, Piggy does not hesitate to speak out in the assemblies when anything important is involved. For instance he speaks with 'bitter realism' about the indiscipline which leads to a large fire, with its threat of uncontrollable power. It is Piggy who points out that the boy with the mulberry-coloured birthmark has disappeared, it is Piggy who tells them that they are behaving 'like a pack of kids', and it is Piggy who damns irresponsibility by considering what the grown-ups would think if they could see how the children are behaving.

Piggy's physical limitations are severe, though; he does not help with the building of the shelters, and his poor sight makes it difficult for him to see anything at a distance. Ralph con-siders 'his fat, his ass-mar and his matter-of-fact ideas were dull', yet he has the same passionate attachment to civilization and the same thought of being rescued as Ralph. He risks physical reprisal, and shouts,

'You and your blood, Jack Merridew! You and your hunting! We might have gone home –' (IV. 67).

One of his weaknesses, as we might guess from his corpulence, is food. He cannot resist the temptation of having meat, but, although he eats with Jack, his principles urge him to a silent protest at the next meeting, when Ralph is to try and put things straight to the boys so that they understand their responsibilities. Piggy tells the assembly that there is no beast – he is essentially down to earth – and suggests that the real fear in them is their fear of people. Again this is pathetic, for Piggy is by now very frightened of Jack. But he is right; his forward-looking imagination sees things very clearly as they will be. He tells Ralph (he is talking about Jack):

'I been in bed so much I done some thinking. I know about people. I know about me. And him. He can't hurt you: but if you stand out of the way he'd hurt the next thing. And that's me' (V. 89).

This is virtually what happens, but it is important for another reason. Piggy is aware, none better, of his own limitations and fears. All the more surprising then that he should determine to face Jack after the latter has stolen his spectacles. Before they set off there comes a moment for Piggy which is probably the proudest of his life:

'You must carry it.'
'When we're ready I'll carry it –'
Piggy sought in his mind for words to convey his passionate willingness to carry the conch against all odds (XI. 163).

Piggy's words are brave, and Ralph's giving him the conch, which they all regard with reverence, is a compliment, a mark of his acceptance by the civilized. Just before his death he makes an impassioned appeal to the savages, this despite his fear and trembling of being struck or of falling. But Piggy is not completely honest. He has witnessed the murder of Simon, yet he tries to explain it away as an accident, and to minimize his part in the ritual. The pathos which surrounds him is heightened by his death. He is blind, helpless, fearful, – and he is struck down senselessly.

Piggy is older than his years because circumstances have made him so, and his faults are directly traceable to his health and his physique. He represents the rational element of mankind who are not acceptable because the truths they tell are unpalatable to the rest, and they are rejected on some excuse – their colour or race, their creed or politics, or even their personalities. In Piggy's case, physical unattractiveness is a further excuse for rejection. He is indeed a 'true, wise friend' for his practical knowledge, his understanding of people and his unswerving sense of right were employed to avert catastrophe.

Simon
'What else is there to do?'

In his Third Programme discussion with Frank Kermode, William Golding said of Simon, 'The illiterate person knows about saints and sanctity, and Simon is a saint'. If we did not know this, there are sufficient clues in the narrative to underline the quality of Simon's sainthood. He picks fruit for the littluns who cannot reach it, he gives Piggy meat when Piggy has none and incurs Jack's wrath for his pains, and he retrieves Piggy's glasses for him when Jack smacks his head. He goes back through the forest alone to Piggy and the littluns when Ralph, Jack and Roger are hunting for the beast; he tries, though he is inarticulate, to tell the assembly what is fundamentally wrong with them all, and when Ralph and Jack report their discovery of the beast on the mountain-top, he suggests that the only thing to do is to go up the mountain.

Simon is a mystic who has the power of foreknowledge. He tells Ralph that he is sure that he will get back, though he makes no mention of himself. When he thinks of the beast 'there rose before his inward sight the picture of a human at once heroic and sick'. His compassion extends to the dead, and he even frees the parachute from the rocks. He loves his fellows, though he frequently cannot express what he wants to say. (For example, his way of showing his affection for Ralph is shyly to stroke his arm.) Many mystics and prophets have been subject to faints and hallucinations, and Simon's greatest (recorded) visionary experience is with the Lord of the Flies. He recognizes the devil, evil, the fundamental disease of man; and he resists temptation, the temptation to say and do nothing. He has seen the killing and the bestiality, and he has discovered what the beast really is. He goes down, staggering, near exhaustion, to be murdered by savages. The parallels with Christ will have been noted, though his name is from Peterkin in *The Coral Island*. It is often the experience of prophets and mystics not to be heeded by their fellows. Simon is despised by Jack for his constant faints, and, like Piggy, he is accepted only by Ralph and the twins. When he tries to speak there is jeering from the assembly; yet he is the only boy on the island who selflessly serves others, from the building of the shelters to his despairing crawl out of the forest into the circle of savages.

William Golding has sufficiently defined Simon, though critical speculation will doubtless continue, but such is the subtlety of his presentation that we do not question his existence. His only noticeably boyish trait is his mock pushing and fighting with Ralph when they first explore the island. But we accept Simon because he is 'batty', because his very oddness is the mark of an individual. Simon going to his small 'cabin' which looks out on the clearing is as real and immediate as Jack placing the pig's head on the stick, as Roger rolling the rock that kills Piggy, as Ralph falling on the beach, hands upraised for mercy. Simon is a life, as well as a symbol.

Roger
The possibilities of irresponsible authority.

There is not much that needs to be said about Roger, but what there is contributes to our understanding of *Lord of the Flies*. Roger develops in the course of the novel from a sardonic, rather quiet boy into the henchman of the Chief, though once again we feel the potential of evil in him early on. When Roger watches Henry, a littlun, playing with the 'tiny transparencies' on the beach, he throws stones which are calculated to miss. We are overtly told that 'Roger's arm was conditioned by a civilization that knew nothing of him and was in ruins'. When he sees Jack approaching 'a darker shadow crept beneath the swarthiness of his skin'. The reason for this is obvious. Jack represents the world of hunting and the prospect of killing – the promise of release from the civilized codes. This promise is to be abundantly fulfilled. It is Roger who accompanies Ralph and Jack in their search of the mountaintop for the beast, tasting excitement and the possibility of blood; it is Roger who follows Jack's frenzy in the mime-rituals of killing. This leads to his assuming the role of chief guard at the fort, and torturer-in-chief to the tribe. Roger is sadistic and irresponsible. He releases the rock which kills Piggy. 'High overhead, Roger, with a sense of delirious abandonment, leaned all his weight on the lever' (XI. 172).

When the tribe return to the fort Roger comes down and we are told that 'The hangman's horror clung round him'. As Jack prods the bound twins, Roger observes,

"That's not the way'.

Roger edged past the Chief, only just avoiding pushing him with his shoulder. The yelling ceased, and Samneric lay looking up in quiet terror. Roger advanced upon them as one wielding a nameless authority (XI. 173).

Later they testify that Roger is 'a terror'. In Roger we see the emergence of latent instincts and tendencies – the type of bestial behaviour which, in our own time, was licensed by the Chiefs who ran the concentration camps during the last war.

Minor characters and littluns

Their heads clustered above the trunks in the green shade; heads brown, fair, black, chestnut, sandy, mouse-coloured.

These are clearly defined but do not merit detailed investigation. Samneric, the twins, are loyal to Ralph until they are taken by the tribe and tortured by Roger. Even after this Sam manages to give Ralph a piece of meat. Like so many of the other biguns, Bill deserts to Jack at the offer of meat and hunting. Robert is always prepared to take part in savagery, and on one occasion is nearly killed during a mime. Maurice is of the same calibre, with fears ingrained in him from the adult world.

The first littlun to appear is Johnny, full of self-confidence, and Phil, another one, later gives an account of the littluns' fears of the beast. The most pathetic is Percival, with his incantation, which disappears as the civilized behaviour of the boys fades, while Henry, in his self-absorption, shows how they are capable of passionate interest when the night fears are banished. The littluns, like Piggy, are helpless; they are a poignant demonstration of man's unwillingness to provide for man or to care for the weak.

Style and structure

There are several facets in the style of most great authors, and in *Lord of the Flies* it would be true to say that there are several styles. Perhaps the most outstanding feature is the incidence of metaphor, the finely economic word-picture much more a part of poetry than of prose writing. These metaphors or images are frequently in connected sequences, as in the description of the fire which gets out of hand in Chapter Two, where the animal images strongly suggest the animal behaviour of the boys later in the novel. One imagery sequence extends throughout the novel, and this is particularly subtle in its underlining of what the boys have exchanged for civilization; even the casual reader will be aware of the subliminal effect. Those are the images which recall the commonplaces, or even luxuries, of home, or domestic comfort and security; the end of sunlight is like the light going out, birds sitting on rocks are like icing on a cake, a rock is as big as a tank or motor-car, the horizon is a taut wire, all these serve to emphasize what has been taken for granted, what is no longer available to see, or touch, or feel. The implication is, perhaps, that when these things are lost, the spiritual and moral bases of the society which knew them may be lost also.

Close to the metaphorical and purely descriptive passages is the factual – geographical, geological, or scientific – phrase or sequence which somehow balances or rounds off the poetry. The best example of this in the novel occurs at the end of Chapter Nine, where the body of Simon is carried out to sea. What is particularly impressive here is Golding's investiture of the fact with a poetry of his own, so that the statement of the cosmic and terrestrial becomes sublime. Another result of these statements is to reinforce the realism of the conception; the naming of a plant or a rock gives actuality, particularly if it is casually done and does not degenerate into a text-book description. Another feature of the style is the ability to convey atmosphere (almost always by metaphor or, in the case of the storm that coincides with the murder of Simon, by repetition); sound (by onomatopoeic words, some self-coined); by the emphasis on certain colours, whether they be in the background (the red rocks) or the foreground (the black caps and cloaks of the choirboys).

Rhythm is also employed frequently in the creation of atmosphere. Thus the single words or short phrases of Ralph as he is pursued in Chapter Ten not only reflect his state of mind but also his breathlessness, his near exhaustion, and even his difficulties in reasoning. In complete contrast, the rhythms of the sentences used at the beginning of Chapter Four suggest by their movement the routine on the island to which the boys become accustomed, while the sentences which describe the 'mirages' fluctuate in length and emphasis, as if in some curious way their verbal differences are a type of distortion. In these rhythms William Golding makes style reflect mood or outlook, and a limpid fluency tells of Simon gathering fruit for the littluns, while the sentences describing the movement of the sea unroll like the power of the tide.

One of the most natural things in *Lord of the Flies* is the dialogue. The slang is of its time, but the voiced thoughts of the children are of any and all time. The reader is struck by the fact that the exchanges in the assemblies have the ring of truth; sometimes one gets the impression of 'practised debators' imitating grown-up manners of delivery in order to be the more impressive. More subtly, the dialogue is used to emphasise traits of character; Jack's manner of speech is quick and jerky, reflecting the impetuous and irresponsible activity of which he is capable, and into which he is to lead the other boys. Piggy's speech indicates the logical nature of his thoughts, Ralph's of his reason, Simon's few words and breaking off, his essential shyness and timidity. But even when they are not in assembly the dialogue of the children is accurately recorded. In the first chapter there is a striking instance of this when Ralph gives Piggy an account of his background, and Piggy tells of his auntie and the sweetshop – the difference in class and speech habits, in confidence and diffidence, is apparent from the actual words spoken. We should observe, too, the way the boys, and particularly the twins, finish each other's sentences off for one another. The savages with the Chief use a different form of speech – a weighted, game-playing utterance in keeping with the way they view their altered status. Perhaps best of all – and this is, of course, linked with rhythm – is the chant of the boys, with its variants, which so superbly expresses the frenzy of mood.

As the student reads *Lord of the Flies* he will realize how concisely written it is. It has been noted how the dialogue fits mood, character, background in civilization, and how it gives way to a formal utterance once the tribe becomes a tribe and ceases to be a group of society-conditioned boys. The student should also note the economy of description, that use of the right word to achieve the desired effect. If we think back over the novel there is no sequence we could wish to omit – everything is relevant, everything is inter-related. Occasionally William Golding uses a technique which is commonplace in film production – the flashback sequence which illumines the past of a character or characters. Such a sequence occurs in Chapter Seven, when Ralph dreams of a particularly happy period during his earlier childhood. This kind of return is part of the structure of the novel, and reinforces the constant meta-phorical echoes of home. Otherwise the narration is a straight-forward progression in time, from the boy's discovery of one another after the landing, to the arrival of the naval officer. For convenience the novel may be divided structurally into three sections.

1 The arrival, and the period immediately afterwards, in which the island is a kind of paradise (with metaphorical sug-gestions and associations with the Garden of Eden and inno-cence).

2 The beginning of the break-up of their own hastily erected society on the island, the differences of outlook, the arrival of the 'beast' from without and, so to speak, from within.

3 The throwing off of civilization by the majority, which leads to murder, persecution, bestiality and the practice of primitive rites.

The conclusion is integral to the novel, though the arrival of the naval officer, and his attitude to what he sees, may be – indeed has been – variously interpreted.

Notes

Chapter 1
The sound of the shell

The opening chapter of the novel describes the coming together of the various boys who have been plane-wrecked on an island in the Pacific. Ralph, who is later to be the elected leader of the boys, meets Piggy, a fat asthmatic boy, and they discuss their situation. Apparently they were evacuated from England when an atomic war began, and the aircraft in which they were travelling was fitted with a detachable passenger-tube. This was released by the aircraft, which has flown off in flames. The tube has smashed into the jungle, but there has been a heavy storm which has carried trees and tube out to sea. The island has a lagoon, the shore is 'fledged with palm trees', and there is a coral reef.

The first significant happening is the discovery of a conch. No grown-ups being available, some symbol of authority is needed in their place. The conch supplies this, thanks to the imagination and practical good sense of Piggy. He instructs Ralph in the correct manner of blowing the conch, and the result is the appearance, singly or in groups, of the boys. After the arrival of the twins, Jack Merridew appears with the choir, who are later to become his hunters. When all the survivors are present and have given their names, there is a vote as to who shall be the leader. Ralph is acclaimed by all except the choir, and immediately propitiates Jack by giving him the choir (already his by coercion) to act as his particular agents. Jack determines to make them hunters.

Ralph announces that he, Jack and Simon will explore the island. Piggy wishes to go, but has to remain and take names on Ralph's orders. They make their way through the undergrowth to the top of the mountain, and, looking down, can confirm that they are on an island. They are able, in their exhilaration, to lever a large rock over the edge and into the forest. From the top they can see the scar in the forest where they landed, and they can see also the platform jutting into the lagoon with the minute figures of the other boys on it. They exult in the pride of ownership – it is *their* island. But as they go down they find a piglet caught in some creepers. Jack does not kill it and the others know why; it is 'because of the enormity of the knife descending and cutting into living flesh; because of the unbearable blood'.

bath of heat Note this, the first of many metaphors which convey the intense humidity of the island, and help to make the feelings and the reactions of the boys real.

the Home Counties The counties of South-East England around London.

wind-breaker A short jacket with a zip-fastener.

lodgements firm positions, footholds.

the delight of a realized ambition i.e. pleasure at being free from any adult supervision.

contours outlines.

flinked Golding has an exquisite ear for words, and coins his own for sound or atmospheric effect. This word has both onomatopoeic and colourful suggestions. (See also Chapter Eight, p.129, and note p.47.)

bow-stave The wooden part of the bow, here used metaphorically to define the curve of the beach.

perspectives relationships between visible objects viewed from particular points.

Twelve years and a few months Note Ralph's age. He is two years younger than Peterkin Gay in *The Coral Island*.

a mildness . . . devil This is important to our understanding of Ralph, and underlines the contrast with Jack.

returned . . . machine-gunned Piggy This description stresses Ralph's boyishness, but also ironically reveals the violence of man which is to become emphatic in this group of small boys.

effulgence radiance, shine.

palm-fronds foliage which grows from the trunks of the palm-trees.

decorous excitement 'Decorous' means dignified and decent. There is a suggestion here that Piggy, who is not boyish, is containing himself because he has something important to say.

conch The shell of a mollusc. In Roman Mythology the Tritons (a race of sea-gods) used conches as trumpets, and they are also used as instruments of call in Hindu temples and on West Indian plantations.

fulcrum lever.

embossed in relief, standing out on the surface.

diaphragm The muscle in the lower part of the chest, which contracts and expands when a person breathes in and out respectively.

fluking up an octave i.e. going higher purely by chance. But observe the onomatopoeic quality of 'fluking'.

scuttered Appears to be a synthesis of scattered and scuttled. Again onomatopoeic.

wubber An onomatopoeic word to convey the falling noise.

digit i.e. finger.

the hot, dumb sand Notice how expressive the word 'dumb' is. The noiseless approach of the children adds to the tension.

the men with megaphones Presumably those who were controlling the evacuation or, more likely perhaps, those who directed the children into the detachable tube.

the eye was shocked ... duplication Shocked, because it seems impossible to the sight. The twins are so alike that it appears almost as if the eyes are lying, or do not see accurately.

Their bodies ... were hidden by black cloaks The choir come from a cathedral school. Notice how Jack (who later says that he is 'chapter chorister and head boy') has regimented them, and how they continue to exist as a unit throughout the book.

hambone frill This is really the paper ornament on a ham-knuckle, but here it refers to a frilled collar commonly worn by choirboys.

sensing his sun-blindness Having been marching in the blazing sun, Jack cannot see at once in the subdued light on the protected platform and its surroundings.

Merridew, his eyes staring This is the first reference to Jack's lack of balance. Later in the novel his eyes are described as having 'that opaque look'.

Gib Gibraltar. **Addis** Addis Ababa, capital of Ethiopia. These places were stops for the aircraft which was evacuating the boys.

at matins over the precentor i.e. at morning service. The precentor is the member of the clergy in general control of musical arrangements in a cathedral, ranking next to the dean.

This last piece of shop Gossip or news of interest only to those who already know about it, in this case the choirboys.

perched like black birds Notice the references to black (already a child's shadow is like a bat). Black is the colour of certain religious orders. It is also the colour of evil.

This was the voice of one who knew his own mind This statement carries an ironic overtone. Jack knows that he wants to hunt, knows he wants to be chief, knows how to sacrifice to the beast, etc. He constantly reveals that his mind is not open to sensible suggestion.

a closed circuit of sympathy A metaphor from civilization to emphasize Piggy's isolation.

chapter chorister Jack has probably won a scholarship presented by the Cathedral to an outstanding choirboy.

This toy of voting Note how the word 'toy' underlines the fact that these are little boys imitating adult practice.

Suffusion i.e. Jack's blush of mortification.

togs clothes.

a hut of straight hair Note the vivid economy of the metaphor.

bumbling Mr Bumble is the name of the corpulent beadle in *Oliver Twist*. It is perhaps an obvious word to apply to a fat boy. Piggy stands irresolute, probably muttering.

rose of indignation Compare this with Jack's blush of mortification.

magicked out of shape or sense Not distorted by mirages or false glamour.

The forest minutely vibrated A reference to the animal life within – pigs, birds, small creatures, insects.

thread through them like pliant needles i.e. needles that will bend. Notice how this simile is linked with *laced*.

Immured in these tangles i.e. imprisoned by the creepers.

the solumn communion of shining eyes i.e. a serious sharing of their delight.

under-dusk i.e. the half-light. The trees and foliage are dense.

defiles narrow ways.

the shattered rocks lifted up their stacks and chimneys Notice how this image of contrast – the city with the island not touched by man – might well have come from the consciousness of one of the boys. Similarly, 'The rock was as large as a small motor car'.

The assault on the summit *Lord of the Flies* was probably written in the year of the Everest Expedition (1953). The phrase has become a commonplace to describe that achievement.

Sway back and forth, catch the rhythm The sentence structure approximates to the movement.

The great rock loitered . . . the island was still A fine descriptive sequence in which the actual rhythm and timing of the fall is made vivid and immediate. Compare it with the description in Chapter Eleven of the action which kills Piggy.

lip of a cirque, or a half-cirque the edge of a hollow on the mountain.

The coral was scribbled . . . finished The whole effect of this indicates the vastness of nature as compared with the smallness of man (even with his atomic wars). It is one of many such images.

they felt . . . steadily astern This illusion springs from the fact that the island is boat-shaped. Ironically, making a boat, even later, does not occur to them. Compare this with *The Coral Island*.

a twining line An imaginary line of string which would indicate the route back.

they savoured the right of domination. They were lifted up: were friends All ironic, in view of their coming experiences.

coign Normally coign of vantage – a place affording a good view.

candle bushes Note the reactions of each of the boys towards this discovery.

the enormity of the knife descending Boys have played make-believe games, but this is the reality of killing.

Chapter 2

Fire on the mountain

Ralph summons an assembly, and reports that they are indeed on an island. They describe the encounter with the piglet – this underlines the need for hunters – and establish the rule that the speaker must hold the conch. Piggy points out to the assembly the realities of their situation, and a little boy is induced to hold the shell. He wants to know what is going to be done about the snake thing or beastie. This makes a serious impression, despite Ralph's attempts at reassurance. Jack says that if there were a beast they would hunt it and kill it, and Ralph then gets to the major point – their need to be rescued. He tells them that they must have fire, and there is an immediate reaction; the assembly disperses – to the disgust of Piggy – following Jack in search of wood.

Jack and Ralph find themselves working together, and a great collection of dead and decaying trees is made. The twins add armfuls of dried leaves to the pile. Now comes the embarrassment of lighting the fire (no-one has the practical sense of Jack Martin in *The Coral Island*) until Jack has the idea of using Piggy's glasses. The fire starts, but collapses. Enmity between Piggy and Jack is now obvious, but the latter wins the approval of the assembly by offering to let his hunters be responsible for keeping the fire going. Piggy takes the conch and begins to speak with 'bitter realism'; as he does so, he notices that part of the forest is aflame. The fire lit by the boys has got out of hand, and must be allowed to burn out. Piggy retains the conch, and points out the need for them all to put first things first. They need shelters, they need a proper fire; he also notes that the boy with the mulberry-coloured birthmark has disappeared. Creepers in flames scare the littluns, for they look like snakes. The 'good' island, the paradise, is beginning to recede.

Wacco. Bong. Doink Notice how the slang is used to convey the reactions of children who are faced with a situation which requires adult action and appraisal.

paler than before and breathless Piggy's asthmatic condition is emphasized (and not only by him), whenever his feelings or physical actions are involved.

The breezes . . . like kittens Unobtrusive images like this point the contrast between the island and home.

'Treasure Island' – 'Swallows and Amazons' – 'Coral Island'
The mention of three children's classics – adventure stories divorced
from realism – carries its own irony.

warped out . . . publicity i.e. not standing upright, but leaning or
dragging back because the focus of attention is upon him.

induced persuaded.

dubiety that required more than rational assurance i.e. the
littluns are so doubtful and apprehensive that mere reasoning cannot
convince them of the truth.

it turned into them things like ropes . . . branches The effect of
this on the littluns is seen when the creepers catch fire at the end of
the chapter. The power of association and suggestion here looks forward to Ralph's own nightmare about the bus centre (Chapter Ten,
p.156).

he lost his thread This is characteristic of Ralph. His ability to
organize his thoughts and keep them on the same track diminishes
later.

Acting like a crowd of kids Again the irony is apparent, but this
also indicates that Piggy is, at least mentally, more mature than the
rest. There is pathos too in the fact that Piggy is not physically
capable of dashing off to look for wood.

errant erring, having faults.

martyred expression We should probably use the commonplace
term 'long-suffering'.

The shameful knowledge . . . confession The sudden seriousness
of the tone suggests that each fears a loss of face before the other if he
cannot light the fire; the suggestion is surely that many people
undertake wrong actions out of pride and persist in
wrong-headedness in order to maintain a kind of false status.

You'll break the conch Apart from the pride of his discovery, Piggy
regards the conch, which represents order and authority, as sacred.

a great beard of flame A vivid metaphor, one of many in this
sequence. i.e. a river of sparks, a clean flag of flame flying, a savage
arm of heat.

the taut wire of the horizon A finely observant metaphorical
description, used two or three times in the novel.

After all, we're not savages . . . best at everything The irony
here is that Jack should be the speaker, for he – very English
in the stiff-upper-lip tradition – becomes the most savage of the
boys.

virtuous recrimination He considers that he can reprimand the
others, because he has the sense to know what should be done.

Small flames . . . shake the mountain Golding is a poet, and this
is another metaphorical sequence rich in associations and suggestions,
'scrambled up like a bright squirrel' . . . 'the fire . . . began to gnaw'
. . . 'as though they were a kind of wild life' . . . 'crept as a jaguar
creeps on its belly.' The spread of the fire causes Ralph to feel 'the
beginnings of awe', and no wonder. It is beyond the control of the
boys before they realize it. The powerful implication is that the fear
and savagery inherent in the boys, once released, will spread just as
rapidly and dangerously. The *drum-roll* of the fire in the forest is
equivalent to the ritual dance and chant of the later boy-killers.
Moreover, the 'splendid, awful sight' has the same kind of
compulsion – it frightens yet it draws.

pall cloak, mantle of smoke over the island.

Chapter 3

Huts on the beach

Some time had elapsed (though we are not told how long), and
Jack is hunting. After a frustrating day, he returns to find
Ralph and Simon struggling to build shelters. Two shaky ones
have been erected, and one is in ruins. Already the ideal society
has broken up. The hunters are out all day searching, and the
littluns and the remaining biguns would rather play than
build shelters. Already the two opposing ways of tackling life
on the island are apparent. Jack wants only to hunt and kill;
Ralph wants shelter and rescue. They are on the point of
openly quarrelling, when Ralph talks of the fears of the littluns,
and Jack confesses that sometimes when he is alone hunting
he feels as if he is 'being hunted'. Ralph contemplates the
smoke, wondering if it is big enough to be seen out at sea; Jack
looks up the mountain too, exultant that he has discovered

where the pigs rest. Again there is the threat of head-on coll-
ision. Meanwhile Simon, whom they all consider queer, having
helped the littluns to the fruit they want, follows the path into
the forest until he comes to a thickly matted spot looking out
on an open space in the jungle.

a tendril pendant from a node a point on the branch from which
the creeper hangs.

seemed bolting and nearly mad Golding constantly refers to
Jack in this way, thus emphasizing his potential for irrational action.

a harsh cry . . . abyss of ages For a moment we have been taken
back to the time when man hunted to survive.

ape-like This is linked to the previous image – Jack is being
compared with prehistoric man by suggestion.

a castanet sound From the Spanish 'castaneta', a hardwood or
ivory instrument, used in pairs to rattle in time with dancing.

Snakes . . . mentionable They are ashamed of expressing fear.
They do not wish to be classed with the littluns.

The opaque . . . eyes again A reflection of his lust to kill, at present
limited to the killing of pigs.

the rub of feeling Ralph and Jack are amazed that their feelings
are so strong.

two continents . . . unable to communicate The image, while it
suggests vast space, also suggests the vast differences of temperament
and standards of the two boys.

his eyes so bright . . . gay and wicked Compare this view of
Simon with the description of Peterkin Gay in *The Coral Island*.

Flower and fruit . . . outstretched hands The harmony of nature
is contrasted with the already apparent disharmony between the
boys. Notice that Simon here is the embodiment of the good
Christian, feeding the weaker and less able. The lush description
gives the effect of life going on everywhere regardless of man.

the creepers . . . foundered ships i.e. ships which have gone
aground with their rigging down.

susurration whispering. An unusual word. We get the impression
that Simon is very much aware of his own heart-beats.

Their green sepals the whorls of leaves forming the outer cases of the buds. This is not merely acute observation on the part of the writer. It is a stress on the normal and permanent in nature which contrasts with the unnatural, nightmarish reactions of the boys.

Revision questions on Chapters 1–3

1 Describe the first reactions of Ralph to his situation on the island.

2 What does the conversation between Ralph and Piggy reveal of the character of each?

3 What impression do you get of Jack when he arrives with the choir?

4 Show how Ralph reveals his sense of responsibility in the first chapter.

5 Compare and contrast the reactions of Ralph, Jack and Simon during their first exploration of the island.

6 Give an account of the main subjects discussed at the first assembly following the return of Ralph, Jack and Simon.

7 Describe the making of the fire and the way it spread.

8 What indications are there in Chapter Two that the boys will not be able to live together harmoniously?

9 Outline the differences between Ralph and Jack which are apparent in Chapter Three.

10 What opinion have you formed of Simon? Give reasons for your answer.

Chapter 4
Painted faces and long hair
The boys gradually get used to the pattern of the days on the island, avoiding the heat, seeing mirages when they fail to avoid it and spending tortured nights. The littluns lead a

'passionately emotional and corporate life' playing on their own for the most part. They build castles, and are occasionally interfered with by biguns like Maurice. Roger spends some time throwing stones near, but not too near, a littlun called Henry, who is inspecting the minute creatures which are washed up on the beach.

Jack has the idea of disguising himself so that the pigs will not sense him when he is hunting. He uses white clay, red, and charcoal, and is so transformed that he does not recognize himself. His success is the turning point in the novel. The mask he has made changes him, for he is 'liberated from shame and self-consciousness'.

Meanwhile Ralph, Simon and Piggy discuss matters. Piggy is full of ideas, most of which Ralph does not take seriously. Ralph is brooding after a swim, when he suddenly sees smoke on the horizon. Piggy can see no smoke from their own fire on the mountain, and when Ralph and the others get to this fire they find that it has gone out. It is a moment of agony. Just then they see the hunters, who should have kept the fire going, returning with the gutted carcase of their first killing, a pig. Jack is full of boasting, but is soon made to realize the extent of his crime. There is a direct confrontation between Ralph and Jack:

> The two boys faced each other. There was the brilliant world of hunting, tactics, fierce exhilaration, skill; and there was the world of longing and baffled common-sense.

Jack hits Piggy and breaks his glasses. He behaves with an 'English' sense of decency, and apologizes for letting the fire out. Ralph resents what he knows to be a 'verbal trick'. He remains silent while the fire is relit. The pig is roasted, and Jack recounts the details of the hunt and the killing. There is a re-enactment of the scene, with Maurice as the pig. The ritual of killing, real or parody, is now part of their lives. Ralph, disgusted, announces that he is calling an assembly.

whelming engulfing, overwhelming.

opalescence colours of white or blue with red, green and yellow reflections.

run like raindrops on a wire Once again, an image from civilization.

extinguisher a hollow conical cap used for putting out a candle.

the Northern European tradition of work the routine of working, relaxing and eating as observed in England, i.e., with set times for doing certain things.

peaked pinched, sharp-featured, sickly.

generic general, as applied to a class or group.

corporate life individuals forming a life together.

a complex of marks a complicated pattern.

dropped in This phrase is used two or three times to describe the boys' arrival on the island. Normally it means to come and go casually as a visitor.

questing in Searching.

detritus Matter produced by wearing away.

Like a myriad of tiny teeth in a saw An image which produces a physical effect on the reader; note once more that it is from civilization.

as big as rugby balls Again, an image that might occur to any of the boys.

that token of preposterous time It symbolizes the passage of time, which has seen some generations come and go and civilizations rise and fall.

Here, invisible yet strong . . . and was in ruins Roger cannot throw stones directly at Henry, because he is still under the influence of civilized society, with its punishment of wrong-doing. That civilization has been destroyed by an atomic war, and the irony is that the civilization of these little boys is to be destroyed from within by themselves.

pointed at the centre . . . setter Setters are dogs trained to stand rigid on scenting game

liberated from shame and self-consciousness Jack is now a 'new' person (not subordinate to anybody) and he is free to act as he wants. He does not think of himself as a boy subject to convention; he is now free to kill.

like the velvet on a young stag's antlers The soft downy skin which covers the stag's horn in the growing stage. A stag which is said to be 'in velvet' is not hunted.

We could make a sundial This shows Piggy's practical nature and, pathetically, his longing for rescue.

balm comfort.

The smoke was a tight . . . slowly The image conveys the idea of distance.

bumbling Used earlier to describe Piggy. See note p.26.

Balanced on a high peak . . . indecision The need is for an immediate decision that will lead to rescue. Ralph is too overwrought to be able to make one.

screes slopes near the sea that are covered with small stones.

Simon looked . . . afraid He knows the difference between Ralph and Jack, and senses that it will lead to tragedy.

Simon slushed . . . church Simon is always sensitive to the behaviour of others. Remember that he is a member of a cathedral choir.

vaguely irritated by this irrelevance This emphasises just how far apart Ralph and Jack are in their estimate of priorities.

yet twitched as he said it The implication is that he is appalled and delighted by what he has done. (A few seconds later he is 'laughing and shuddering'.)

His mind was crowded . . . like a long satisfying drink This is to become his obsession. He feels that he must do it again.

Passions beat . . . awful wings Notice that this powerful image is given to Simon, not to Ralph. Simon gets Piggy's glasses back for him, and is almost moved to violence by what Jack has done.

parody i.e. making Piggy ridiculous by imitating him. Notice how Jack has once again 'got away with' something which all know to be wrong.

this verbal trick Jack has apologized, but Ralph resents the fact that the apology meets with the boys' approval. He feels that they should all see that Jack's irresponsibility has cost them the chance of rescue.

By the time the pile . . . barrier Notice how the image is linked with the actual physical labour.

Not even Ralph knew ... fastened elsewhere Ralph and Jack
have hitherto been bound together as leaders; now Ralph and Piggy
are bound together by the wish for rescue and for an ordered,
responsible existence. The action also saves Piggy from any
humiliation. Only Ralph could take the glasses from Piggy without
giving offence.

islanded in a sea of meaningless colour The image powerfully
suggests not only Piggy's visual situation but that of the whole group.

Jack looked around ... respect He wants them to understand
that by getting them meat he has been acting for all of them – it is
an assertion of power following Ralph's recriminations. Instead
Jack gets only the respect accorded to the successful hunter.

One for his nob one blow on the head. These are little boys, not
savages, once again reverting to their slang expressions to convey
their experiences.

Chapter 5

Beast from water

Ralph summons what is to be the most critical assembly since
their arrival. Before he does so, he thinks out their situation,
but experiences occasional lapses in concentration. He realizes,
now, that he has not the same capacity for rational thought as
Piggy. When he addresses the assembly, however, Ralph puts
their responsibilities to them very clearly. He tells them that
they should be prepared to die rather than let the fire out, and
he rules that the fire should be lit only on the mountain. Finally
he deals with fear, and suggests that they talk it out of their
systems.

Jack takes the conch, and immediately attacks the littluns
for their fear. The bully in him undoes all the good that Ralph
has done. He says that there is no beast on the island, and the
assembly applauds him with relief.

Piggy is the next to take the conch, and he says that the
littlun who talked about the beast should be heard. The littlun
talks about the twisty things, and has his experiences interpreted as a nightmare by Ralph. Simon confesses to going out
in the night, and is forbidden by Ralph from doing so again.

The next littlun breaks down completely, and Maurice saves the situation by clowning and leading the minds of the other littluns away from their fears. Then follows the suggestion that the beast comes out of the sea, and an argument about this occurs which seems to Ralph pointless. He feels that things are breaking up again. Simon, temporarily articulate despite his timidity, suggests that the beast is within them; but his point is ruined by Jack. Ralph gets the conch, and there is talk of ghosts. He is made to realise that many of the boys believe in ghosts. The fact that they do moves Piggy to anger, but he is confronted by Jack, who proceeds to flout the rules by speaking out of turn, attacking Ralph verbally, and then breaking up the assembly. Piggy urges Ralph to summon the assembly again by blowing the conch, but Ralph is cautious. Piggy reveals to him that he is scared of Jack, and warns Ralph that Jack hates him. They bewail the fact that there are no adults to help them. The chapter reveals the complete split between Ralph and Jack, and henceforth this division is to lead to savagery and, worst of all, murder.

where every path was an improvization where one adapts oneself according to the circumstances – perhaps losing sight of the important things while doing so. Remember that Ralph has to put to the assembly the important priorities, for most of the boys have revealed their inability to see them.

so that he noticed . . . dirt and decay These are facts, but they also symbolize the dirt and decay within, the corruption of the boys themselves.

wit common sense, intelligence.

apex i.e. where the triangle joined at the top.

like . . . in your hands Not only is this vivid, it indicates Ralph's longing for things he has been used to. It underlines the pathos of the boys' situation.

what was a face? What was anything? The events on the island have so moved Ralph that there are times when he is uncertain of his own standards. Sometimes he cannot think straight. As things get worse, so Ralph has more lapses of concentration.

Piggy intended . . . disapproval Because he is disgusted with the boys for letting the fire out.

like heavy round stones An image from their daily experience – they drop stones into the pool.

I've got the conch Notice how many times this is repeated, and notice also how the responsible boys, like Ralph and Piggy, treat the conch. When he has finished speaking, Ralph sets it down *ceremonially*, and there is an allusion to his reverence for it (see p.78).

You'll be talking about ghosts . . . next Once again Piggy's practical sense is apparent. This is exactly what they do.

Unless we get frightened of people Piggy, with his fear of Jack, has sensed how dangerous and savage people can be.

I saw something moving among the trees The littlun is describing Simon, although he does not know it until Simon confesses. The incident looks forward ominously to Simon's emergence from the trees into the circles of boys who kill him.

He was taken short Jack is adept at making the funny remark which ridicules others – and which also draws the boys away from serious considerations.

trying to pretend he was in a tent Because this would protect him from the glare of publicity in which he finds himself.

the assembly broke into a chant The thoughtless cruelty of this looks forward to the positive action which follows upon the chanting in the ritual killing of pigs – or boys.

a silent effigy . . . the conch An effigy is an image. The reference to the conch is deliberate. Jack is shortly to break the rules by speaking without it.

He yawned and staggered Percival is in a state of near exhaustion, in part brought on by his fears in the night. He falls asleep, later startling Ralph and Piggy when he cries.

sough moaning, whistling or rushing sound.

to speak in assembly was a terrible thing to him Simon is very sensitive and self-conscious. He would rather help by some action than by having to speak.

Simon became inarticulate . . . illness i.e. the force of evil within man. He seeks to explain this by referring to something dirty, but Jack ruins the effect. The result is the inevitable refuge – laughter.

orgasm violent excitement, paroxysm.

Simon's effort . . . cruelly Civilization, the shelters, their small society have fallen in ruins; and Simon is to be beaten to death by something worse than laughter. These images show how powerfully suggestive is Golding's writing.

Two grey trunks . . . noticed by day The heightened reactions of the boys makes the supposed change vivid and immediate to them.

The world . . . was slipping away Ralph is annoyed by the belief of the boys in ghosts. He realizes their capacity for belief in anything; and it seems to him that capacity means the end of rational influence.

Or animals? Or savages? What's grown-ups going to think? Piggy is clearly conscious of right and wrong, and also of the way things are developing. The reference to grown-ups shows their most pathetic need and the naval officer who lands on the beach to rescue them reveals what he thinks should have been done by 'British' boys.

We'll close in and beat and beat This is now Jack's creed – the killing is the most significant thing that has happened to him and has imprinted itself on his judgement and his imagination.

discursive rambling. Usually applied to an argument or way of reasoning.

the incantation . . . help him He is almost certainly having a nightmare. Percival has obviously been told to state his name and address – probably he first did it when Piggy went around collecting names (or when he was evacuated) – but no ordinary statement of facts can protect him from his dreams.

Chapter 6

Beast from air

While the children are asleep, a sign does come from the world of grown-ups – a parachutist from an air-battle falls, and is dragged to the mountain-top. He is dead. Next morning the twins awake, talk about the previous evening's events, and re-light the fire which is practically out. Then they see the figure of the parachutist, and believe that it is a beast. They rush down to tell Ralph and the others. It is still dark, but when dawn comes an assembly is summoned. The twins tell their story – it is, of course, elaborated and distorted, so that the beast they saw is given claws and teeth, and it followed them through the trees. Jack wants to go and hunt the beast immediately, but Ralph has to organize things. There is another argument between Ralph and Jack, but Ralph triumphs and plans the day's action against the beast. They set off – Piggy is minding the littluns – and first of all search the tail-end of the island where even Jack has not been before. Ralph goes ahead, although he is frightened, but is joined by Jack. Jack experiments with a rock which could be toppled over a ledge, and, while Ralph is reasoning, the boys play at pushing the rocks over. Once again a sense of purpose and responsibility has deserted them. Jack wants to make a fort of the place – in effect he does later – but Ralph insists on going on.

Waxy Slang for 'angry'.

the scurrying woodlice These cannot avoid being burnt alive, just as the boys cannot avoid being caught up in the savagery of Jack and his followers.

the plopping noise of fabric blown open This would give the impression not only of noise (which a beast would almost certainly make) but also of movement.

flailing acting like a flail, which is a hand threshing implement.

interminable Here it means that the dawn is a long time coming.

but then he hesitated and did not blow Because the threat of the beast is made definite by the account of the twins – it might be attracted to them by the sound of the conch.

the growing slice of gold i.e. the sun.

the rest of the boys ... curiously This would seem to be because their hostility is now evident, and not just due to what the author earlier calls the 'rub of feeling'.

like what's its name Presumably a reference to the character o' Tarzan, created by Edgar Rice Burroughs.

uncomfortably embroiled Uneasily caught up in the argumen' between Ralph and Jack.

Piggy let out his breath . . . creeping around his lips Piggy has realized the intensity of the crisis, and this brings on an asthmatic attack.

Jack trod with theatrical caution Obviously enjoying the role of leading the hunt and pretending – or perhaps feeling – that an encounter with the beast is imminent.

there rose before his inward sight . . . sick i.e. heroic because brave, but sick because mentally deranged. In view of his long experience with Jack and his ways, he may well have Jack in mind.

pressure of personality form of self-consciousness which makes inarticulate.

constrainedly restraining his natural feelings. He is obviously absorbed in his thoughts.

returned to his personal hell Ralph has denied the possibility of a beast, and now has to live with what appears to be the reality. Moreover, there is the thought of the coming physical encounter with it.

Soon, in a matter of centuries Apparently a contradiction, but time is relative. According to the actions of nature, soon. 'A matter of centuries' contrasts with the actual life-span of the boys.

the breathing of some stupendous creature . . . breathed out The great natural power of nature is stressed here – this is greater than that of any beast, and Ralph's appraisal of this force in fact calms him.

polyp kind of animal of low organism, i.e. hydra.

clutch set of eggs hatched at one time.

The taut blue horizon See note on 'the taut wire of the horizon'. p.29.

millwheel a wheel, especially a water-wheel, used to drive something.

Something flittered like a bat's wing This shows what a strain Ralph is under, and how he is now finding it difficult to keep his grip on standards that he knows to be right. Fortunately, the irresponsible actions of the boys with the rocks restore his mental perspective.

Mutinously, the boys fell silent An ominous indication that they are going to reject Ralph.

Chapter 7

Shadows and tall trees

The search for the beast continues, and Ralph dreams. He longs to be clean, and contemplates the dirt of the hunters, and then the prospect of the island from a new angle. Simon tells him that he will get back all right – he means back home – but Ralph tells him he is 'batty' – the usual epithet applied to Simon's behaviour. Ralph dreams again of his happiest home times as they press on. He is roused by a charging pig, and throws his wooden spear at it, tasting for some moments the delight that Jack has experienced in his killing. For a time he thinks the boar he has struck is the beast they are after, but Jack soon corrects him. They talk excitedly, and then Robert pretends to be the pig. The ritual begins, with Ralph joining in. Robert is nearly killed, and the chant has almost made the mime reality. They now decide to explore the mountain to see if the beast is up there. They reach the higher slopes, and Ralph decides that someone must go back to Piggy and the littluns. Simon volunteers. When they come near the top, Jack decides to go alone. Ralph joins him, and they in turn are joined by Roger. They reach the burnt patch, then Jack leaves them. He reappears to tell them that he has seen something on the top. Ralph goes to investigate, with Jack and Roger. They see something 'like a great ape', and flee.

clipped blue ... like shining hair Notice how these images are used as Ralph looks at the sea from the other side of the island, shortly after thinking about his need for cleanliness, a haircut, etc.

an arm of surf ... fingers of spray A running-on of the image.

obtuseness bluntness. Here it means with no relief or change.

I just *think you'll get back all right*. The words are italicized for emphasis. Simon has a faith which Ralph cannot grasp, and he repeats his statement three times. Simon's assertion that Ralph will get back seems to suggest, however, that he (Simon) may not. The term 'batty' is the boyish substitute for failure to explain his mysticism.

Jack bent down to them as though he loved them A sufficient indication of his lust to kill. It also shows how easily he is distracted from what he has to do.

Once . . . good-humoured and friendly The day-dream is the natural refuge for one in Ralph's position. But note how many significant facts about his earlier life are revealed, and how they help to explain his character and attitudes.

scrabbled scratched or groped about. Strong onomatopoeic suggestion.

felt that hunting was good after all Because he has achieved some success at it. But note the temptation involved, and the fact also that he is accepting, temporarily, Jack's standards.

Like Berengaria The wife of Richard-Coeur-de-Lion, who once saved his life by sucking a wound made by a poisoned arrow.

The circle moved in and round The ritual is becoming more organized. This 'game' with Robert as the pig nearly leads to murder – it is only just short of the final stroke, which was such an 'enormity' in the beginning.

to get a handful of that brown, vulnerable flesh Notice how a normal boy like Ralph has been affected by the ritual.

we could do it properly As indeed they do, when they come to murder Simon. Irony.

Use a littlun This sounds like a joke, but the suggestion is that Jack would indeed use a littlun if he had to, or even if the mood took him.

Vividly he imagined Piggy by himself This is because he has to reason things out, and he now knows that the real thinker among the boys is Piggy.

a queer, tight voice Jack hates Piggy, and one of the reasons is that Ralph likes him, or at least protects him. Jack thus cannot bully Piggy as he would wish. Moreover Piggy really stands between compromize, or even friendship of a kind, between Ralph and Jack.

seeing him, infuriatingly, for the first time Simon has set off to go back to Piggy, and Ralph realizes that Jack thinks of no-one but himself, and is incapable of responsible feeling for others.

out of the new understanding that Piggy had given him i.e. that Jack hates him, and that he will hurt him if he can.

as though something indecent had been said This is typical of boys' reaction to anything emotional which causes embarrassment.

displaced Because he is now at the rear, not the leader.

pricked round the head of a mountain i.e. made minute holes in the sky.

save where the mountain ... blackness A vivid image. Golding uses unusual combinations of words to achieve a sudden effect.

A kind of 'plop' noise Obviously the fabric of the parachute.

a kind of dentist's chair unreality Ralph's reason tells him that there is no beast at the top, and he feels as if he is having a dream at the dentist's under the influence of gas. Soon he will wake up.

Green lights of nausea Having unexpectedly touched the ashes – and being overwrought and fearful – Ralph suddenly feels sick.

the top of the mountain was sliding sideways The effect on him of sickness and dizziness.

diminishing, moving mountain Not only the feeling of sickness, but the sense of movement against the vast spaces of the sky.

He bound himself ... stood up A supreme effort of will-power on Ralph's part. Hating the nameless beast will give him the courage to move.

Revision questions on Chapters 4–7

1 Describe the routine of life on the island.

2 Account for Jack's actions and Ralph's reactions in Chapter Four.

3 By close reference to Chapter Four, show that the society of the boys is beginning to break up.

4 Give an account of Ralph's thoughts before he addresses the assembly in Chapter Five. How has he changed?

5 Contrast the attitude of Ralph and Jack towards 'the fear'.

6 Describe the roles played by Piggy and the littluns at this assembly.

7 Give an account of the boys' actions after the twins tell them about the beast.

8 What evidence is there in Chapter Six of the irresponsibility of the majority of the boys?

9 Show how the author deepens our understanding of Ralph in Chapter Seven.

10 Describe what actually happens on top of the mountain.

Chapter 8
Gift for the darkness

Ralph reports back to Piggy and the rest; inevitably, he distorts what he has seen. Jack calls an assembly. He launches an attack upon Ralph, saying that he is not a proper chief and that he is like Piggy. He asks the assembly in effect, to make him chief; there is no movement from the boys, and Jack goes off saying that he is 'not going to play any longer'.

The assembly continues with Simon surprisingly taking the conch and suggesting that they climb the mountain. There is no response. Then Piggy suggests making a fire where they are, since they can no longer have it on the mountain. They build one near the platform. When they pause to rest they realise that many of the biguns have gone off. Piggy tries to reassure Ralph by saying that they can do without them. Then he and the twins bring him fruit for a feast. At this point they begin to think about Simon. He has gone to his natural cabin in the forest.

Meanwhile Jack is organising the boys who have come to him. The hunt begins, and eventually a large pig is killed. Jack decides to sacrifice the head of the pig to the beast. This is stuck on a stick in the clearing, and Simon is a silent witness. Back near the platform Ralph and Piggy have a discussion about why things break up, when suddenly they are attacked by Jack and his savages. Jack announces that he is going to have a feast, and says he may be prepared to let *them* take part in it. When they have gone Ralph calls a meeting, once more stressing the importance of the fire. Afterwards they think about the meat that the others are having.

Simon, still in his sheltered spot, is being harangued by the head on the stick, the Lord of the Flies. Simon's hallucination, for this is what it is, is a striking demonstration of the power of evil.

Jack was kneeling He is so obsessed that he draws again the circle which the boys make when they are attacking a pig.

The beast had teeth Ralph cannot help but distort.

Boys armed with sticks But note his realism here. The irony is that these boys can quickly turn into savages.

his age-old tremors in the forest When he felt that something was following him. But 'age-old' suggests that it seems a long time ago, with time measured in terms of experience.

He isn't a prefect In his determination to convince the assembly, Jack is using a standard of judgment that carries weight for him and for the other boys, but only within the context of their experience in the past at school.

full of shame Jack's appeal is emotional, and cannot succeed because the boys are too ashamed openly to disown Ralph. Their silence hides their real feelings. Many of them do desert to Jack quickly.

I'm not going to play any longer Supreme pathos. He is once again a little boy who has not got his own way in a game. Irony too, because the results are terrifying.

A half-sound of jeering Notice that Simon is never accepted by anyone except Ralph and Piggy.

derisive incomprehension Piggy completely fails to understand, because he does not possess Simon's capacity for self-sacrifice.

Only Piggy could have the intellectual daring This is the opinion of the assembly (now that Jack has gone). It reinforces our knowledge that Piggy is the most practical boy on the island.

there was a partyish air about the gathering In view of how soon 'the gathering' is to break up, this is a little ironic. Compare it with Jack's invitation to his feast, and also with Piggy and the twins pathetically collecting fruit for Ralph 'for a feast kind of'.

I expect they won't play either Piggy has a cutting irony of his own at times.

as if in sympathy with the great changes among them Again, this appears to be from Ralph's consciousness, and reflects his sensitivity.

the arrow of the sun There is, of course, the implication that Simon is affected by the sun, and that this produces his hallucination – the monologue addressed to him by the Lord of the Flies.

their voices had been the song of angels The choir has a deep-rooted loyalty to Jack. The memory of their voices is an intentional contrast with their unpleasant savage potential now.

their tormented private lives Their fears, and the emergence of these fears in nightmares.

We'll kill a pig ... the kill for it Jack is adopting the methods of primitive societies.

wore the damp ... old clothes Just as he has got used to the filth of his clothes (compare his attitude with that of Ralph) so he has got used to the primeval scene, and can thus be expected to behave in a primeval manner.

wedded to her in lust The lust, of course, for blood (and meat) which is to be the motivating force of their immediate existence.

struck down by the heat The conception of tropical heat as being a blow is a favourite one of Golding's.

from an unknown world i.e. the world of man.

The butterflies still danced, preoccupied We can guess from this that it is the clearing on which Simon looks out; more important, perhaps, is the word 'preoccupied'. It suggests that while murder is occurring eyes can be shut to it – precisely what happens later with Ralph and Piggy as Simon is killed.

flinked Remember the innocent usage of this word, p. 24, and compare it with the suggestion now.

rubbed the stuff over his cheeks Primitive celebration of the killing rite. They are closely drawn together by this sharing of the blood they have made.

they looked suddenly furtive They have done what they have never done before – and what, in a world of grown-ups, they would not dare to do.

It's a gift Obviously to appease the beast, who will not attack them if satisfied.

All at once they were running away Not merely because they have done what they should not have done. This is the *real beast* – and we remember how Ralph and Jack and Roger ran from 'the ruin of a face'.

the infinite cynicism of adult life The eyes convey to Simon the positive evil of which man is capable, i.e. destruction of his race, either in an atomic war, or here on the island.

I know that Simon voices his thoughts aloud. He has sensed before that the evil is within.

A little headache Simon has had the sun on him for some time, but he has just seen the ritual killing of the pig. The hallucination that the head is addressing him now becomes more important than fact.

buzzed like a saw An expressive, onomatopoeic simile.

iridescent showing colours like those of the rainbow.

the Lord of the Flies Beelzebub (Arabic: Baal-Zebub, the fly-lord) is one of the manifestations of the devil. Simon recognizes it for what it is, the fundamental evil, the evil within man shown by this killing.

thunder went off like a gun There are many suggestions that a storm is coming – and it is timed to coincide with the climax of savagery among the boys.

an aimless little pattern ... fingers Compare this with the meaningful circle that Jack made earlier with his forefinger (VIII. 118).

the cloud canyons Vividly conveyed noise, again contributing to the atmosphere of the storm's build-up. Notice that Jack and his savages sway for a moment when they hear the noise.

The group of boys looked ... respect It is the symbol of their civilized attitude as distinct from Jack's savagery – after all they must have something to show instead of the paint and the 'fun'. Notice too 'The Chief has spoken' – so much part of the game of ritual, and so menacing when one thinks of what his orders could lead to. Notice that Ralph feels 'the need for ritual' when they have their small assembly.

the shutter that flickered in his brain i.e. the strain he is under. This image, together with that of the curtain, expresses the blockage in the clarity of his thought processes.

You are a silly little boy This is a temptation to Simon to forget or ignore the discovery he has made. After all, everyone else considers him silly.

You like Ralph . . . and Jack? This would be an odd combination if it were not Simon who is apparently being addressed. The latter is the embodiment of Christianity (love thy enemies), and here there is a parallel with Christ being tempted in the wilderness.

Pig's head on a stick These are the only words Simon utters during this sequence. They represent his clinging to sanity, his resistance to temptation.

the parody of laughter The laughter is in Simon's head. And it is a parody because it is not good healthy laughter, but mockery. See note on 'parody', p.35.

I'm part of you The beast, the presence of evil, is within us all.

He knew that one of his times was coming on Simon has always been subject to fainting fits, and everything is conspiring to bring one on – the sun, the killing of the pig and the presence of the head, the thundery atmosphere, his own realization and the courage he is going to need to take any action.

You know perfectly well you'll only meet me down there i.e. in the bestial and evil behaviour of the other boys. In view of what happens, this is a terrifying piece of irony.

Simon was inside the mouth This is the illusion before he faints. It anticipates his own death.

Chapter 9
A view to a death

Simon bursts a blood-vessel in his nose and then falls asleep. Meanwhile the clouds continue to build up over the island. Simon goes up the mountain to see the beast. He frees the parachute from the rocks, and then staggers down the mountain to tell the others what the beast on the top was.

First of all Samneric and Bill go to Jack's party, and they are followed by Ralph and Piggy, who pretend that they are unmoved by the feasting and ritual. But as some of the boys rush away from the fire with the meat, they bump into Piggy and knock him down, and the ensuing laughter draws them all together. Jack asks who is going to join his tribe, and immediately there is trouble with Ralph. They argue, and the storm begins. Piggy tries to draw Ralph away, and with the next thunder-roll Jack urges them all to dance. At first Roger is the pig, then he becomes a hunter and the centre of the circle is empty. Lightning strikes, the circle becomes a horseshoe, and Simon crawls out of the jungle into it. Simon is slaughtered, and after the killing, the wind lifts and carries the parachute and its burden out to sea. The chapter ends with a beautiful, mystical description of Simon and the carrying of his body out to sea.

A view to a death A reminiscence from the hunting-song *John Peel*.

revolving masses . . . to explode This is commonplace scientific explanation, but it helps to make the coming scenes real.

the cannon i.e. the thunder.

the flies explode from the guts with a vicious note A striking description which captures the sudden noise and movement.

What else is there to do? i.e. he can confirm only that the beast does not exist on the mountain, and he must return to the others with this news.

with a sort of glum determination like an old man Not only his exhaustion. Simon is old in experience and in intuitive knowledge, much older than any of the other boys.

the mechanics of this parody i.e. how this imitation of a beast worked.

colours of corruption various shades of decay.

from the wind's indignity from being buffeted by the wind.

I got a pain in my head Another indication of the intensity of the pre-storm atmosphere.

I mean – to make sure nothing happens Piggy's weakness is, of course, his appetite.

bourdon This is from the French, and means a low-pitched stop on the organ. Here it refers to the noise of the sea.

Piggy once more was the centre of social derision The
unpleasant truth is that people are warmed by laughing at someone
else.

not with calm . . . violence A reference to Jack and the savages as
well as the coming storm.

authority . . . like an ape He is moved to assert himself. The image
suits Jack, who has become a kind of ape-man.

the conch doesn't count at this end of the island Irony again.
Their behaviour demonstrates that they have rejected what the
conch stands for.

this demented but partly secure society Made crazy by fear, the
ritual and the storm, but secure because all are together.

Him! Him! Note that Simon's arrival, in fact, probably stops the
killing of the littlun who has broken the circle of the biguns.

Simon was crying out something about a dead man on a hill
The words suggest the crucifixion; with tragic irony, Simon dies
that others may live.

the tearing of teeth and claws The only possible image to convey
the bestiality of the boys.

the parachute filled . . . and out to sea Notice that with the
death of Simon the 'beast' goes; but there is to be more sacrifice to
the beast in man's heart.

The beast lay huddled Notice the superb irony in the references
to Simon as the 'beast'.

a dimple of tension . . . an inaudible syllable The beauty of the
description is the prelude to Simon's being received into nature – his
death seems the less tragic because of the order and harmony of
which he is to become a part. From *moonbeam-bodied creatures* to the
end of the chapter is the finest writing in the book. The mystical
conception – or is it all merely the accident of light? – is informed
by a comprehensive sense of the relationship of things. Note
particularly the last paragraph of the chapter, which contains a
statement of fact put in such a way as to stress the inevitability and
permanence of cosmic and terrestrial things. Simon's body moves
out to sea; we feel, in the words of Shelley, 'He is made one with
Nature'*.

* *Adonais. An elegy on the death of John Keats*, Stanza XLII.

Chapter 10

The shell and the glasses

Ralph, dirty, limping and battered, comes out of the coconut trees and makes for the platform where Piggy awaits him. Samneric and a few littluns are the only ones left who have not defaulted to Jack's camp. Ralph and Piggy talk by the platform which has witnessed the useless assemblies, and where 'the fragile white conch still gleamed by the polished seat'. They both know that Simon has been murdered, and that they took part in the ritual killing; Piggy tries to pretend that they were all scared, or that it was an accident, as if this absolves them from full responsibility. Their shame urges them to hide the facts from Samneric who, when they appear, are ready with their own excuse – 'we got lost last night'. The depth of their self-knowledge and fear is succinctly put: 'Memory of the dance that none of them had attended shook all four boys convulsively'.

Meanwhile, the Chief is exercising his power by beating Wilfred without apparent cause, thus giving his sadistic henchman Robert time to consider 'the possibilities of irresponsible authority'. The Chief, secure behind his white and red blocked face, details some of his tribe for defence, warns against the possibility of attack from the others, and reminds them that the beast has attacked them once 'disguised'. One of the tribe, Stanley, suggests that they have killed the beast, but he is overruled by the Chief, who thus strengthens his own position, for as long as the beast is alive warriors are needed to combat it. He also stills the half-feelings of guilt which are present. He solves the problem of fire by planning to raid the other camp, obviously with the intention of taking Piggy's glasses.

Back at the other camp the four boys try to keep their fire going, Ralph with an eye to comfort as well as rescue. Sam and Eric began to despair and Ralph, though he finds difficulty in concentrating ('that curtain flapped in his head and he forgot what he had been driving at'), still preserves some optimism. However, he gives up the uneven battle with the fire before nightfall. The boys crawl into their own shelter, and Ralph finds that his dream of home suddenly becomes a nightmare in which he is dancing around the lamp-standard in a bus centre, while a bus crawls out of the bus station, 'a strange bus'. Piggy awakes, and tells Ralph that they will be all 'barmy' if they aren't rescued. Just after this they are attacked, and in the ensuing chaos Ralph and Eric fight one another, thinking they are battling with the raiders. When the latter have gone they find that Piggy's glasses have been taken, but the conch has been left, untouched, by the chief's seat. Jack has proved his power – 'He was a chief now in truth'.

gazing with impaired sight at the chief's seat They are not seeing clearly because their eyes have filled with tears at the thought of Simon's death and their own part in it.

He took the shell caressingly He holds it in this way because it represents for him the rule of sanity and order which contrasts so poignantly with the present state of savagery to which they have all been reduced.

He was shivering The next few lines of dialogue reveal why. Ralph is still obsessed by Simon's murder.

searching for a formula This is a set form of words or definitions, a rule which can be, perhaps unintelligently, followed. The irony here is that there is no given explanation which can exonerate Piggy from his part in the killing, no definition which can soften or alter the fact.

Ralph shuddered at the human contact Again, because of his human contact with Simon during the dance around him.

The air was heavy with unspoken knowledge Everything around them knows of their guilt.

obscene word The word 'dance' has come to mean this for them because of the killing.

assimilating the possibilities of irresponsible authority Roger sees how Jack is using his power as chief, and probably sees himself acting on his own initiative i.e. with the rock that kills Piggy.

The semicircle Note that the boys have become a tribe, sitting in the primitive manner and position of tribesmen.

Half-relieved . . . the savages murmured again They are half-relieved because Jack is telling them that they have not killed the beast (i.e. Simon) and half-daunted because they fear the coming battle with the beast.

give it the head Jack reminds his hunters of the necessity to sacrifice to the beast by leaving the head on a stick.

A theological speculation presented itself This leads on from the previous statements. Jack here thinks of the beast as a god, perhaps controlling their destinies.

a flaw of wind A squall of wind or short storm.

dredged in The verb appropriately conveys the effort of will needed on Ralph's part to remember the world outside the island.

carrying their spears, saying little, cramming in haste Obviously because they fear an attack, either from a beast or from Jack's tribe.

that curtain . . . driving at This is the image used to convey Ralph's loss of concentration, and is an indication that he too could go the way of Jack and his tribe (as indeed he had done the previous evening). The curtain shuts off reason and sanity.

But the attraction of wildness had gone When the boys first came to the island it was wild, but seemed to be a paradise. Ralph is conscious of the change and the reality, and thinks determinedly of something ordered and civilized, i.e. a town.

There was a bus . . . a strange bus A clever re-enactment of the killing of Simon, showing what a deep effect it has produced on Ralph. He is having a nightmare, and Piggy wakes him.

tendrils of hair This is a subtle use of image. Tendrils are creepers; the forest is full of them, and we remember that the littluns associate them with snakes.

his body jumped and twitched This shows how near hysteria is Ralph.

ambushed by sleep Again a suggestive use of metaphor.

A composite of these things The beast, Simon, the bus, etc.

smothering finality (The shelter) appeared to smother everyone inside it completely.

purged cleansed.

the bow-stave of beach A metaphorical description used earlier in Chapter One, p.10. See note on 'bow-stave', p.24.

occasionally they turned cartwheels Note that Golding does not let the reader forget that they are little boys indulging in their own ritual of triumph.

Revision questions on Chapters 8–10

1 Say why, in your opinion, the boys do not decide to follow Jack immediately when he tries to usurp Ralph's chieftainship.

2 Describe the effect of Jack's departure on Piggy.

3 What is the importance of Simon's dialogue with the Lord of the Flies?

4 Outline the effects used by the author in Chapter Nine to create atmosphere.

5 Describe the various manifestations of savagery in the boys.

6 What do you find in Chapter Nine that could be described as 'poetic?'

7 Describe the reactions of Ralph and Piggy to the killing of Simon.

8 What actually happens when Jack, Roger and Maurice raid Ralph, Piggy and the twins?

Chapter 11
Castle rock

Ralph tries to light the fire, and then calls an assembly, attended, pathetically, by himself, the twins, Piggy and a few littluns. Piggy announces that he is going to Jack to ask for his glasses back, because 'right's right'. Ralph says that they will accompany him and, to Piggy's pride, tells him that he must carry the conch. They set off in a small procession, Piggy being guided by the others. They make for Castle Rock, and Ralph leads the way up, Piggy all the time in fear and trembling because he cannot see. When they get near Ralph blows the conch to summon an assembly. Jack appears behind him, and Ralph demands Piggy's glasses back, calling Jack a thief as he does so. Jack attacks him with his spear. There is a short encounter, then they break off – each a little scared of the other – and Ralph makes his last attempt to talk reason to the savages. Meanwhile Jack orders his tribe to capture the twins, and this is done. Ralph, incensed, attacks Jack; Piggy, holding the conch, intervenes. He reasons, and, as he does so, Roger levers a large rock free from above. This hits Piggy, and he goes over the cliff on to a rock forty feet below, and then into the sea. Ralph is attacked, but escapes. The Chief goes back to the fort with his prisoners, and Roger takes over their torture.

luminous wall of his myopia The latter word means short-sightedness. Piggy can see only light and colour – he cannot make out shapes and forms.

as on that first morning ages ago In point of time, not long. In point of experience and changes, a very long time.

Then there was, there was Ralph cannot quite bring himself to refer to the murder of Simon.

We could smarten up a bit and then go ... A pathetic attempt to put them on terms with the savages by showing them how civilized he (Ralph) and his group are.

I'll show him the one thing he hasn't got He believes, rightly, that Jack wants absolute power and that he resents anything which could undermine his authority.

The shape of his old assembly ... listened to him A superb imaginative feeling for immediacy. Piggy is, in fact, declaiming as if to a large audience.

something that Simon had said to him once, by the rocks 'You'll get back all right. I think so, anyway' (VII. 106).

I knew that The preceding dialogue shows just how overwrought Ralph is. He very nearly picks a quarrel with Piggy. All this springs from the need to assert his chieftainship over the few who still respect it – even Ralph wishes to cling to the little power that he has.

The twins ... for the first time They have not known him assert himself in this way before. The think they see into the real person. Ralph felt the same about Jack when he allowed Simon to go back alone through the forest to Piggy and the littluns (VII. 112).

like a blade that has been scoured A knife that has been cleaned and made bright.

luminous veil Again a reference to the fact that Piggy can see only colours, not objects.

Some source . . . in Roger's body He has a sense of power because of the height, because of the rock which he can lever over, and because the stone that he has just thrown has shown how dangerous is the position of those beneath.

You aren't playing the game Notice how Ralph uses the language of schoolboy society to those who are no longer boys – they have become savages. Remember also that Jack once said that he didn't want to 'play any longer' (VII. 121).

shivering, silvery, unreal laughter This appears to be the laughter of evil spirits or demons. There is a suggestion too of mockery and insanity about it, at least as seen from Ralph's sane standpoint.

out of the heart of civilization From the standards they have been used to, for they have been caught at a disadvantage, unfairly.

You're a beast and a swine and a bloody, bloody thief One cannot help but notice that this is not merely the language of a schoolboy – it carries a certain irony in view of the part the beast has played in their lives on the island, and the way pig-killing has become the major part of existence for Jack and his tribe.

the talisman, the fragile shining beauty of the shell The badge or symbol. There is real pathos in this final description of it in its entirety.

delirious abandonment giving himself up happily to.

His head opened . . . turned red Notice that this is description from a distance. Its economy makes it more powerful than close description.

like a pig's after it has been killed Irony (and remember the name Piggy). Roger has demonstrated how little value the savages place on human life.

the sea breathed again in a long, slow sigh An effective personification. Compare the way the sea takes Piggy with the way it takes Simon.

The hangman's horror clung round him He has 'executed'
Piggy – he is a killer and to be feared.

A nameless authority The authority to torture. He considers
Jack's methods inadequate, and in view of what the twins have just
seen him do, they have every reason to look up in 'quiet terror'.

Chapter 12
Cry of the hunters

Ralph is nursing his wounds and hiding. He goes back to the
fruit and eats, wondering why two littluns run away from him
when they see his battered appearance. In the evening, he
creeps back towards Jack's end of the island. He finds himself
in a clearing looking at the remains of a pig's head on a stick.
Hysterically he smashes the skull, and returns to the thicket in
front of Castle Rock. He hears the tribal ritual, and sees that
Samneric are now guarding Castle Rock against him. He
attracts their attention and they tell him that he is going to be
hunted – like a pig – the next day. They add that Roger has
sharpened a stick at both ends. Ralph cannot grasp the significance of this. Sam gives him a piece of meat.

Ralph sleeps in a thicket, and rouses the next morning to
hear the savages signalling to one another. The hunt gets
nearer, and Ralph realizes that one of the twins, under torture,
has given him away. From the top a rock is released at him,
then another. The savages come near, and Ralph wounds one
with his spear. There follows the narrowing of the hunt as
Ralph runs this way and that. The forest has been set on fire,
and Ralph, fleeing from flames and spears, ends up on the
beach, begging for mercy.

When he looks up he finds that a naval officer is gazing down
at him. Rescue has come, and Ralph breaks down in his
anguish.

that indefinable connection between himself and Jack i.e. the
fact that he has been chief means that Jack will have to kill him in
order to establish his chieftainship permanently.

It was an accident It is surely ironic that he should use the words that Piggy used to describe Simon's murder (X. 149).

looked steadily at the skull . . . had done The effect of the light and the contrast – the symbol of evil and the symbol of good – contribute to the irony.

The skull regarded Ralph . . . Compare this with its effect on Simon.

'I've got pax.' 'I'm immune'. The irony is, of course, that Jack, having refused to play Ralph's game, is not playing *any* game now.

accepted this new fact like a wound As it is, obviously, to his battered spirit.

the water breathed . . . whiteness The rock on which Piggy fell. Yet in a way the image is one of peace.

while the vivid stars . . all ways The sensation of height and his own exhaustion probably combine to produce this effect.

antiphonal alternately.

ululation howling, hooting.

Roger sharpened a stick at both ends The significance does not strike Ralph. It can mean only that Ralph's head will be displayed on a stick stuck into the ground just as the pig's was – another sacrifice to the beast.

the slow spilt milk . . .below The many references to the rock in this chapter seem to indicate, as indeed the next few lines do, how ever-present Piggy is in Ralph's mind.

if the horrors of the supernatural emerged Ralph, who has just been compared to a littlun, is frightened of being alone.

ensconce establish.

diddle thwart (slang).

the top of the thicket . . . gigantic hand Compare this image with the earlier ones of the giant and the leviathan.

as a cottage, as a car, a tank Again images from civilization.

like an outsize steamroller Another such image.

showed his teeth . . . snarled a little Notice how Ralph is adopting the mannerisms of the savages.

crepitation crackling sound.

to dread the curtain . . . brain How many times has he temporarily lost the power to reason? Now he feels the coming loss of sanity.

Break the line From now on in the narrative Golding uses Ralph's own thoughts to convey the fear and the movement and the tension from time to time. Frequently this takes the form of Ralph's self-urgings.

You'll get back Simon's words repeated in his mind – a shred of faith in the agony of this hunt.

He shot forward ... snarling, bloody Compare this with the description of the first sow killed (VIII. 128-9), or with the noises made from time to time by the savages.

someone's legs were getting tired He is almost dissociated from himself in his terror.

epaulettes The ornamental shoulder-pieces of a uniform.

Fun and games Almost every remark and conclusion of the officer carries the author's irony – adult incomprehension of what has happened.

an incantation that had faded clean away A minor emphasis on how quickly things implanted by civilization are erased.

a pack of British boys Notice how this phrase echoes Jack's much earlier assertion of their superiority (II. 42). 'Pack' has its own irony.

Like the Coral Island Irony again.

the end of innocence, the darkness of man's heart When they had come to the island it had been a paradise, but the evil within them had transformed it.

the true, wise friend called Piggy Note that there is no mention of Simon. Ralph was drawn to Simon, but did not understand him. He came to respect Piggy, however, as having a greater practical intelligence than he had.

Revision questions on Chapters 11 and 12

1 What do you learn of Piggy and Ralph in Chapter Eleven?

2 Give a brief account of Roger's role in the events which lead to Piggy's death.

3 How does the author convey to the reader Ralph's reactions during the various stages of his pursuit by the savages?

4 Describe, in some detail, the manifestations of savagery in Chapter Twelve.

5 What is the effect of the arrival of the naval officer?

6 Describe, in your own words, why Ralph breaks down, despite the fact that the rescue he so much wanted has come.

Questions

1 State what you consider to be the main themes of *Lord of the Flies*.

2 Write a description of the island, indicating clearly where the events of importance occur.

3 Give an account of the most *frightening* incident in the novel, and show how Golding achieves the necessary atmosphere.

4 Describe the attitude of the various boys towards the conch during the course of the novel.

5 State whether or not you consider the ending of *Lord of the Flies* a fitting climax to the novel, giving the reasons for your decision.

6 Write a character-sketch of Ralph. What, in your opinion, does he represent?

7 By a close study of Jack's actions, show how he becomes obsessed by hunting and killing.

8 Indicate the various steps in the development of the friendship between Ralph and Piggy.

9 Do you find Piggy a pathetic character or not? Give reasons for your answer.

10 What is the attitude of the various boys towards Simon? Try to account for their opinions by some study of the character of Simon.

11 Do you find the characterization of *Lord of the Flies* true to life? Give your reasons.

12 Do you consider that *Lord of the Flies* is a searching examination of human nature? Give reasons for your opinion.

13 In what ways do the littluns reflect the 'fear' which dominates the lives of the boys on the island?

14 Do you think that boys in this situation would behave as these do? Give reasons for your answer.

15 Show, by direct reference to the text, how the author's ear for dialogue helps in the characterization of the boys.

16 Do you consider *Lord of the Flies* optimistic or pessimistic in its implications? For what reasons?

17 'A beautiful and desperate book.' Would you agree with this estimate of *Lord of the Flies*? Give reasons for your answer.

18 By close reference to the text, indicate the main aspects of Golding's style.

19 Select *two* passages from the novel which you consider to be beautiful, and show how the author achieves his effects.

20 What is, for you, the most outstanding quality of *Lord of the Flies*?

Pan study aids Titles published in the Brodie's Notes series

W. H. Auden Selected Poetry

Jane Austen Emma Mansfield Park Northanger Abbey Persuasion
Pride and Prejudice

Anthologies of Poetry Ten Twentieth Century Poets
The Metaphysical Poets The Poet's Tale

Samuel Beckett Waiting for Godot

Arnold Bennett The Old Wives' Tale

William Blake Songs of Innocence and Experience

Robert Bolt A Man for All Seasons

Harold Brighouse Hobson's Choice

Charlotte Brontë Jane Eyre

Emily Brontë Wuthering Heights

Robert Browning Selected Poetry

John Bunyan The Pilgrim's Progress

Geoffrey Chaucer (parallel texts editions) The Franklin's Tale
The Knight's Tale The Miller's Tale The Nun's Priest's Tale
The Pardoner's Tale Prologue to the Canterbury Tales
The Wife of Bath's Tale

Richard Church Over the Bridge

John Clare Selected Poetry and Prose

Samuel Taylor Coleridge Selected Poetry and Prose

Wilkie Collins The Woman in White

William Congreve The Way of the World

Joseph Conrad The Nigger of the Narcissus & Youth
The Secret Agent

Charles Dickens Bleak House David Copperfield Dombey and Son
Great Expectations Hard Times Little Dorrit Oliver Twist
Our Mutual Friend A Tale of Two Cities

Gerald Durrell My Family and Other Animals

George Eliot Middlemarch The Mill on the Floss Silas Marner

T. S. Eliot Murder in the Cathedral Selected Poems

J. G. Farrell The Siege of Krishnapur

Henry Fielding Joseph Andrews

F. Scott Fitzgerald The Great Gatsby

John Osborne Luther

Alexander Pope Selected Poetry

Siegfried Sassoon Memoirs of a Fox-Hunting Man

Peter Shaffer The Royal Hunt of the Sun

William Shakespeare Antony and Cleopatra As You Like It
Coriolanus Hamlet Henry IV (Part I) Henry IV (Part II) Henry V
Julius Caesar King Lear King Richard III Love's Labour's Lost
Macbeth Measure for Measure The Merchant of Venice
A Midsummer Night's Dream Much Ado about Nothing Othello
Richard II Romeo and Juliet The Sonnets The Taming of the Shrew
The Tempest Twelfth Night The Winter's Tale

G. B. Shaw Androcles and the Lion Arms and the Man
Caesar and Cleopatra The Doctor's Dilemma Pygmalion Saint Joan

Richard Sheridan Plays of Sheridan: The Rivals; The Critic;
The School for Scandal

John Steinbeck The Grapes of Wrath Of Mice and Men & The
Pearl

Tom Stoppard Rosencrantz and Guildenstern are Dead

J. M. Synge The Playboy of the Western World

Jonathan Swift Gulliver's Travels

Alfred Tennyson Selected Poetry

William Thackeray Vanity Fair

Flora Thompson Lark Rise to Candleford

Dylan Thomas Under Milk Wood

Anthony Trollope Barchester Towers

Mark Twain Huckleberry Finn

Keith Waterhouse Billy Liar

Evelyn Waugh Decline and Fall Scoop

H. G. Wells The History of Mr Polly

John Webster The White Devil

Oscar Wilde The Importance of Being Earnest

Virginia Woolf To the Lighthouse

William Wordsworth The Prelude (Books 1, 2)

John Wyndham The Chrysalids

W. B. Yeats Selected Poetry

Australian Titles

George Johnston My Brother Jack

Thomas Keneally The Chant of Jimmy Blacksmith

Ray Lawler Summer of the Seventeenth Doll

Henry Lawson The Bush Undertaker & Selected Short Stories

Ronald McKie The Mango Tree

Kenneth Slessor Selected Poems

Ralph Stow The Merry-Go-Round in the Sea To the Islands

Patrick White The Tree of Man

David Williamson The Removalists

Student's notes